Learn Version Control with Git

A step-by-step course for the complete beginner

This book is only possible because of a team of outstanding people.
Thank you Julian, Alex, Chris, Pete, Danny, Heiko, Sam, and Fabricio.

Table of Contents

Introduction   7

About Being Professional 8

About This Book 9

About the Author.. 10

1 The Basics   11

What is Version Control? 12

Why Use a Version Control System? 14

Getting Ready 17

Setting Up Git on Your Computer 18

The Basic Workflow of Version Control 21

Starting with an Unversioned, Local Project 25

Starting with an Existing Project on a Server 28

Working on Your Project 30

2 Branching & Merging 41

Branching can Change Your Life 42

Working in Contexts 43

Working with Branches 47

Saving Changes Temporarily 49

Checking Out a Local Branch 53

Merging Changes 56

Branching Workflows 60

3 Remote Repositories 65

About Remote Repositories 66

Local / Remote Workflow 68

Connecting a Remote Repository 69

Inspecting Remote Data 71

Integrating Remote Changes 77

Publishing a Local Branch 78

Deleting Branches 80

4 Advanced Topics 82

Undoing Things 83

Undoing Local Changes 85

Inspecting Changes in Detail with Diffs 89

Dealing with Merge Conflicts 95

Rebase as an Alternative to Merge 100

Submodules 107

Workflows with git-flow 122

Handling Large Files with LFS 133

Authentication with SSH Public Keys 143

5 Tools & Services 148

Desktop GUIs 149

Diff & Merge Tools 152

Code Hosting Services 155

Closing Thoughts 158

State of Play.. 159

Appendix 160

Appendix A: Version Control Best Practices.................................... 161

Appendix B: Command Line 101... 164

Appendix C: Switching from Subversion to Git 170

Appendix D: Why Git? 175

INTRODUCTION

About Being Professional

What does it take to be a professional? Is it about how much you know? About knowing your topic inside out? Of course it is. But it's only one part of the equation.

The other part is about using the right tools and cultivating the right habits. You won't find a five-star chef who works with a cheap knife - he knows that he will produce better results and work safer with the best tool for the job. Similarly, you won't find a professional tennis player who doesn't train his endurance - he knows that tennis isn't just about hitting the ball across the net.

Just the same, you won't find a top programmer, web developer, or web designer who doesn't use version control. They know that things go wrong all the time in our industry and therefore prepare. They know that collaboration must be as safe & easy as possible because teamwork is paramount in our industry. They know that, when they're working sloppy, they'll have to pay the bill in the end.

Don't mind a little bit of sweat to learn version control. It's a big step on your way to becoming a better professional.

About This Book

The goal of this book is to get you started with version control and Git as quickly and easily as possible. Unlike other books about this topic, this one doesn't require a master's degree in computer science to read it. It's aimed at beginners of programming, at designers, at project managers... It tries not to require too much prior knowledge on the technical side. It tries to go slowly.

That being said, Git and version control in general remain highly technical topics. I can't spare you all of this, but I'll try to explain workflows & backgrounds thoroughly and provide a lot of real-world examples.

Since everyone comes with his own, unique background, it's hard to determine a common starting point for everybody. For this reason, I have provided various basic topics in the appendix:

› In case you're still unsure if you should use Git as your version control system, Appendix D: Why Git? might be worth a look.

› If you're about to switch from SVN, you might find Appendix A: Version Control Best Practices.It gives you an overview of the differences between the two systems.

› Should you need an introduction to working on a command line interface, you should definitely take a look at Appendix B: Command Line 101.

Have fun learning Git!

About the Author

Tobias Günther is the CEO and founder of fournova, a small software startup based in Germany. The company's product Tower helps over 80,000 users in companies like Apple, Google, Amazon, and Ebay to easily & productively work with the Git version control system.

Since many years, Tobias is a regular speaker on conferences large and small for topics related to Git and version control. Additionally, he has written numerous articles and tutorials for blogs & magazines (for example for the "Tower Blog", A List Apart, Smashing Magazine, or SixRevisions).

## CHAPTER 1

THE BASICS

What is Version Control?

You can think of a version control system (short: "VCS") as a kind of "database". It lets you save a snapshot of your complete project at any time you want. When you later take a look at an older snapshot (let's start calling it "version"), your VCS shows you exactly how it differed from the previous one.

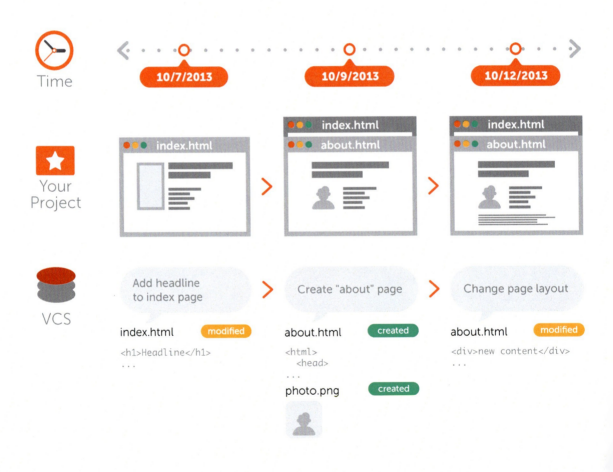

Version control is independent of the kind of project / technology / framework you're working with:

> It works just as well for an HTML website as it does for a design project or an iPhone app

> It lets you work with any tool you like; it doesn't care what kind of text editor, graphics program, file manager or other tool you use

Also, don't confuse a VCS with a backup or a deployment system. You don't have to change or replace any other part of your tool chain when you start using version control.

A version control system records the changes you make to your project's files. This is what version control is about. It's really as simple as it sounds.

Why Use a Version Control System?

There are many benefits of using a version control system for your projects. This chapter explains some of them in detail.

Collaboration

Without a VCS in place, you're probably working together in a shared folder on the same set of files. Shouting through the office that **you** are currently working on file "xyz" and that, meanwhile, your teammates should keep their fingers off is not an acceptable workflow. It's extremely error-prone as you're essentially doing open-heart surgery all the time: sooner or later, someone will overwrite someone else's changes.

With a VCS, everybody on the team is able to work absolutely freely - on **any** file at **any** time. The VCS will later allow you to merge all the changes into a common version. There's no question where the latest version of a file or the whole project is. It's in a common, central place: your version control system.

Other benefits of using a VCS are even independent of working in a team or on your own.

Storing Versions (Properly)

Saving a version of your project after making changes is an essential habit. But without a VCS, this becomes tedious and confusing very quickly:

> How much do you save? Only the changed files or the complete project?
>
> In the first case, you'll have a hard time viewing the complete project at any

point in time - in the latter case, you'll have huge amounts of unnecessary data lying on your harddrive.

› How do you name these versions? If you're a very organized person, you might be able to stick to an actually comprehendible naming scheme (if you're happy with "acme-inc-redesign_2013-11-12_v23"). However, as soon as it comes to variants (say, you need to prepare one version **with** the header area and one without it), chances are good you'll eventually lose track.

› The most important question, however, is probably this one: How do you know what exactly is different in these versions? Very few people actually take the time to carefully document each important change and include this in a README file in the project folder.

A version control system acknowledges that there is only **one** project. Therefore, there's only the one version on your disk that you're currently working on. Everything else - all the past versions and variants - are neatly packed up inside the VCS. When you need it, you can request any version at any time and you'll have a snapshot of the complete project right at hand.

Restoring Previous Versions

Being able to restore older versions of a file (or even the whole project) effectively means one thing: you can't mess up! If the changes you've made lately prove to be garbage, you can simply undo them in a few clicks. Knowing this should make you a lot more relaxed when working on important bits of a project.

Understanding What Happened

Every time you save a new version of your project, your VCS requires you to provide a short description of what was changed. Additionally (if it's a code / text file), you can see what exactly was changed in the file's content. This helps you understand how your project evolved between versions.

Backup

A side-effect of using a distributed VCS like Git is that it can act as a backup; every team member has a full-blown repository of the project on his disk - including the project's complete history. Should your beloved central server break down (and your backup drives fail), all you need for recovery is one of your teammates' local Git repository.

Getting Ready

Command Line or GUI?

There are two main ways of working with Git: either via its "Command Line Interface" or with a GUI application. Neither of these are right or wrong.

On the one hand, using a GUI application will make you more efficient and let you access more advanced features that would be too complex on the command line.

On the other hand, however, I recommend learning the basics of Git on the command line, first. It helps you form a deeper understanding of the underlying concepts and makes you independent from any specific GUI application.

> ⛓ CROSS REFERENCE
> In case the command line is all Greek to you, I've prepared a Appendix B: Command Line 101 in the appendix for you that will show you the most important basics.

As soon as you're beyond the raw basics, you should consider using a GUI application to make your day-to-day work easier and more productive. We highly recommend that you have a look at Tower, the Git client that is trusted by over 80,000 users in companies like Apple, Google, Amazon, IBM, and Twitter.

Setting Up Git on Your Computer

Installing Git has become incredibly easy in recent times. There are one-click installers for both Mac and Windows.

Installing Git on Windows

On Windows, you can download the "Git for Windows" package from here: https://git-for-windows.github.io/

When running the installer EXE, you should choose the default options in each screen. After finishing the installation, you can begin working with Git by starting the "Git Bash" application. You'll find it in the Windows START menu, inside the "Git" folder:

Installing Git on Mac OS

On Mac OS X, a one-click installer package is available that can be downloaded from here: https://sourceforge.net/projects/git-osx-installer/

Once this is installed, you can jump right into Git by starting *"Terminal.app"* on your Mac. You'll find this in the *"Utilities"* subfolder of your "Applications" folder in Finder:

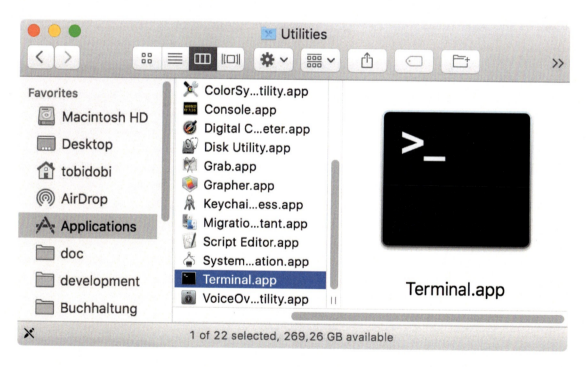

Configuring Git

A couple of very basic configurations should be made before you get started. You should set your name and email address as well as enable coloring to pretty up command outputs:

```
$ git config --global user.name "John Doe"
$ git config --global user.email "john@doe.org"
$ git config --global color.ui auto
```

 NOTE

In this book, like in many others, the "$" sign represents the prompt of the command line interface (you don't have to type this character in your commands!). Therefore, any time you see a line starting with the "$" sign, it means we're executing commands in "Terminal" or "Git Bash".

Again, if this is all greek to you, you might want to look at Appendix B: Command Line 101.

Additionally, I recommend having a Cheat Sheet on your desk(top) so you don't have to remember all the commands by heart.

The Basic Workflow of Version Control

Before we get lost in Git commands, you should understand what a basic workflow with version control looks like. We'll walk through each step in detail later in this book. But first, let's get an understanding of what the workflow in general is like. The most basic building block of version control is a "repository".

> GLOSSARY
> ## Repository
>
> Think of a repository as a kind of database where your VCS stores all the versions and metadata that accumulate in the course of your project. In Git, the repository is just a simple hidden folder named ".git" in the root directory of your project. Knowing that this fol-der exists is more than enough. You don't have to (and, moreover, should not) touch anything inside this magical folder.

Getting such a repository on your local machine can be done in two ways:

› If you have a project locally on your computer that is not yet under version control, you can initialize a new repository for this project.

› If you're getting on board of a project that's already running, chances are there is a repository on a remote server (on the internet or on your local network). You'll then probably be provided with a URL to this repository that you will then "clone" (download / copy) to your local computer.

1. As soon as you have a local repository, you can start working on your files: modify, delete, add, copy, rename, or move files in whatever application (your favorite editor, a file browser, …) you prefer. In this step, you don't have to watch out for **anything**. Just make any changes necessary to move your project forward.

2. It's only when you feel you've reached a noteworthy state that you have to consider version control again. Then it's time to wrap up your changes in a commit.

 GLOSSARY

Commit

A commit is a wrapper for a specific set of changes. The author of a commit has to comment what he did in a short "commit message". This helps other people (and himself) to understand later what his intention was when making these changes.

Every set of changes implicitly creates a new, different version of your project. Therefore, every commit also marks a specific version. It's a snapshot of your complete project at that certain point in time (but saved in a much more efficient way than simply duplicating the whole project…). The commit knows exactly how all of your files and directories looked and can therefore be used, e.g., to restore the project to that certain state.

---

3. However, before you commit, you'll want to get an overview of what you've changed so far. In Git, you'll use the "status" command to get a list of all the changes you performed since the last commit: which files did you change? Did you create any new ones or deleted some old ones?

4. Next, you tell Git which of your local changes you want to wrap up in the next commit. Only because a file was changed doesn't mean it will be part of the next commit! Instead, you have to explicitly decide which changes you want to include. To do this, you add them to the so-called "Staging Area".

5. Now, having added some changes to the Staging Area, it's time to actually commit these changes. You'll have to add a short and meaningful message that describes what you actually did. The commit will then be recorded in your local Git repository, marking a new version of your project.

6. From time to time, you'll want to have a look at what happened in the project - especially if you're working together with other people. The "log" command lists all the commits that were saved in chronological order. This allows you to see which changes were made in detail and helps you comprehend how the project evolved.

7. Also when collaborating with others, you'll both want to share (some of) your changes with them and receive the changes they made. A remote repository on a server is used to make this exchange possible.

GLOSSARY
Local & Remote Repositories

There are two kinds of repositories:

› A "local" repository resides on your local computer, as a ".git" folder inside your project's root folder. You are the only person that can work with this repository, by committing changes to it.

› A "remote" repository, in contrast, is typically located on a remote server on the internet or in your local network. No actual working files are associated with a remote repository: it has no working directory but it exclusively consists of the ".git" repository folder. Teams are using remote repositories to share & exchange data: they serve as a common base where everybody can publish their own changes and receive changes from their teammates.

Starting with an Unversioned, Local Project

Let's start with an existing project that is not yet under version control. Change into the project's root folder on the command line and use the **"git init"** command to start versioning this project:

```
$ cd <path/to/project/folder>
$ git init
```

Now take a moment to look at the files in that directory (including any hidden files):

```
$ ls -la
```

You'll see that a new, hidden folder was added, named *".git"*. All that happened is that Git created an empty local repository for us. Please mind the word *"empty"*: Git did **not** add the current content of your working copy as something like an *"initial version"*. The repository contains not a single version of your project, yet.

 GLOSSARY

Working Copy

The root folder of your project is often called the "working copy" (or "working directory"). It's the directory on your local computer that contains your project's files. You can always ask the version control system to populate your working copy with any version of your project. But you always only have one working copy with one specific version on your disk - not multiple in parallel.

Ignoring Files

Typically, in every project and on every platform, there are a couple of files that you don't want to be version controlled: on Mac OS, e.g., those pesky ".DS_Store" files aren't worth versioning. In other projects, you might have build or cache files that make no sense in a version control system. You'll have to decide yourself which files you don't want to include.

 CONCEPT

Which Files Should I Ignore?

As a simple rule of thumb you'll most likely want to ignore files that were created automatically (as a "by-product"): temporary files, logs, cache files...

Other examples for excluded files range from compiled sources to files that contain passwords or personal configurations.

A helpful compilation of ignore rules for different projects and plat-forms can be found here: https://github.com/github/gitignore

The list of files to ignore is kept in a simple file called ".*gitignore*" in the root folder of your project. It's highly recommended to define this list at the very beginning of your project - **before** making your first commit. Because once files are committed, you'll have to jump through some hoops to get them out of version control, again.

Now, let's get going: Create an empty file in your favorite editor and save it as ".*gitignore*" in your project's root folder. If you're on a Mac, e.g., you'll want to make sure it contains at least the following line:

```
.DS_Store
```

If there are other files you want to ignore, simply add a line for each one. De-fining these rules can get quite complex. Therefore, to keep things simple, I'll list the most useful patterns which you can easily adapt to your own needs:

› **Ignore one specific file:** Provide the full path to the file, seen from the root folder of your project.
`path/to/file.ext`

› **Ignore all files with a certain name (anywhere in the project):** Just write down the file's name, without giving a path.
`filename.ext`

› **Ignore all files of a certain type (anywhere in the project):**
`*.ext`

› **Ignore all files in a certain folder:**
`path/to/folder/*`

Making Your First Commit

With some ignore rules in place, it's time to make our initial commit for this project. We'll go into great detail about the whole process of committing a little later in this book. For now, simply execute the following commands:

```
$ git add -A
$ git commit -m "Initial commit"
```

Starting with an Existing Project on a Server

When you're getting on board of a project that's already running, you were probably given a URL to the project's remote repository on a server. Such a URL can take many forms:

> ssh://user@server/git-repo.git
> user@server:git-repo.git
> http://example.com/git-repo.git
> https://example.com/git-repo.git
> git://example.com/git-repo.git

No matter what format the URL is, you can just pour it into the "git clone" command. However, you should first make sure that you are in the folder where you want this project to be downloaded to:

```
$ cd your/development/folder/
$ git clone https://github.com/gittower/git-crash-course.git
```

 NOTE

In case you don't have any remote repository of your own to experiment with, feel free to clone from the above URL. I'll use this repository in my examples for the rest of this book.

Git will now download a complete copy of this repository to your local disk - on condition that you're allowed to access this repository.
For the *"http"* and *"git"* protocols, no access rights are necessary.

For *"https"* URLs, the command line might ask you for a username and a password.

For *"ssh"* URLs (either with a leading *"ssh://"* or, with the shorter form, *"user@ server..."*), you'll have to use *"SSH Public Key"* authentication. While being very safe, efficient, and widely used, it's also a little bit of work to set up. For detailed information about this topic I recommend taking a look at chapter Authentication with SSH Public Keys later in this book.

Working on Your Project

No matter if you created a brand new repository or if you cloned an existing one - you now have a local Git repository on your computer. This means
you're ready to start working on your project: use whatever application you
want to change, create, delete, move, copy, or rename your files.

 CONCEPT

The Status of a File

In general, files can have one of two statuses in Git:

> **untracked**: a file that is not under version control, yet, is called
> "untracked". This means that the version control system doesn't
> watch for (or "track") changes to this file. In most cases, these
> are either files that are newly created or files that are ignored and
> which you don't want to include in version control at all.

> **tracked**: all files that are already under version control are called
> "tracked". Git watches these files for changes and allows you to
> commit or discard them.

The Staging Area

At some point after working on your files for a while, you'll want to save a new
version of your project. Or in other words: you'll want to commit some of the
changes you made to your tracked files.

THE GOLDEN RULES OF VERSION CONTROL

#1: Commit Only Related Changes

When crafting a commit, it's very important to only include changes that belong together. You should never mix up changes from multiple, different topics in a single commit. For example, imagine wrapping both some work for your new login functionality and a fix for bug #122 in the same commit:

› Understanding what all those changes really mean and do gets hard for your teammates (and, after some time, also for yourself). Someone who's trying to understand the progress of that new login functionality will have to untangle it from the bugfix code first.

› Undoing one of the topics gets impossible. Maybe your login functionality introduced a new bug. You can't undo just this one without undoing your work for fix #122, also!

Instead, a commit should only wrap related changes: fixing two different bugs should produce (at the very least) two separate commits; or, when developing a larger feature, every small aspect of it might be worth its own commit.

Small commits that only contain one topic make it easier for other members of your team to understand the changes - and to possibly undo them if something went wrong.

However, when you're working full-steam on your project, you can't always guarantee that you only make changes for one and only one topic. Often, you work on multiple aspects in parallel.

This is where the *"Staging Area"*, one of Git's greatest features, comes in very handy: it allows you to determine which of your local changes shall be committed. Because in Git, simply making some changes doesn't mean they're automatically committed

Instead, every commit is *"hand-crafted"*: each change that you want to include in the next commit has to be marked explicitly (*"added to the Staging Area"* or, simply put, *"staged"*).

Working Copy
Your Project's Files

 Git watches tracked files for new local modifications...

Staging Area
Changes included in the Next Commit

Local Repository
The ".git" Folder

Tracked (and modified)

 If a file was modified since it was last committed, you can stage & commit these changes

 Changes that were added to the Staging Area will be included in the next commti

 All changes contained in a commit are saved in the local repository as a new revision

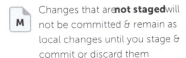

 Changes that are **not staged** will not be committed & remain as local changes until you stage & commit or discard them

Untracked

Changes in untracked files aren't watched. If you want them included in version control, you have to tell Git to start tracking them. If not, you should consider ignoring them.

Getting an Overview of Your Changes

Let's have a look at what we've done so far. To get an overview of what you've changed since your last commit, you simply use the "git status" command:

```
$ git status
# On branch master
# Changes not staged for commit:
#   (use "git add/rm <file>... " to update what will be committed)
#   (use "git checkout -- <file>..." to discard changes in working
#   directory)
#
#       modified:   css/about.css
#       modified:   css/general.css
#       deleted:    error.html
#       modified:   imprint.html
#       modified:   index.html
#
# Untracked files:
#   (use "git add <file>..." to include in what will be committed)
#       new-page.html
no changes added to commit (use "git add" and/or "git commit -a")
```

Thankfully, Git provides a rather verbose summary and groups your changes in 3 main categories:

> "Changes not staged for commit"
> "Changes to be committed"
> "Untracked files"

Getting Ready to Commit

Now it's time to craft a commit by staging some changes with the "git add" command:

```
$ git add new-page.html index.html css/*
```

With this command, we added the new "new-page.html" file, the modifications in "index.html", and all the changes in the "css" folder to the Staging Area. Since we also want to record the removal of "error.html" in the next commit, we have to use the "git rm" command to confirm this:

```
$ git rm error.html
```

Let's use "git status" once more to make sure we've prepared the right stuff:

```
$ git status
# On branch master
# Changes to be committed:
#   (use "git reset HEAD <file>..." to unstage)
#
#        modified:   css/about.css
#        modified:   css/general.css
#        deleted:    error.html
#        modified:   index.html
#        new file:   new-page.html
#
# Changes not staged for commit:
#   (use "git add <file>..." to update what will be committed)
#   (use "git checkout -- <file>..." to discard changes in working
#     directory)
#
#        modified:   imprint.html
#
```

Assuming that the changes in "imprint.html" concerned a different topic than the rest, we've deliberately left them unstaged. That way, they won't be included in our next commit and simply remain as local changes. We can then continue to work on them and maybe commit them later.

Committing Your Work

Having carefully prepared the Staging Area, there's only one thing left before we can actually commit: we need a good commit message

 THE GOLDEN RULES OF VERSION CONTROL:

#2: Write Good Commit Messages

Time spent on crafting a good commit message is time spent well: it will make it easier to understand what happened for your team-mates (and after some time also for yourself).

Begin your message with a short summary of your changes (up to 50 characters as a guideline). Separate it from the following body by including a blank line. The body of your message should provide detailed answers to the following questions: What was the motivation for the change? How does it differ from the previous version?

The "git commit" command wraps up your changes:

```
$ git commit -m "Implement the new login box"
```

If you have a longer commit message, possibly with multiple paragraphs, you can leave out the "-m" parameter and Git will open an editor application for you (which you can also configure via the "core.editor" property).

CONCEPT

What Makes a Good Commit?

The better and more carefully you craft your commits, the more useful will version control be for you. Here are some guidelines about what makes a good commit:

> Related Changes: As stated before, a commit should only contain changes from a single topic. Don't mix up contents from different topics in the same commit. This will make it harder to understand what happened.

> Completed Work: Never commit something that is half-done. If you need to save your current work temporarily in something like a clipboard, you can use Git's "Stash" feature (which will be discussed later in the book). But don't eternalize it in a commit.

> Tested Work: Related to the point above, you shouldn't commit code that you think is working. Test it well - and before you commit it to the repository.

> Short & Descriptive Messages: A good commit also needs a good message. See the paragraph above on how to "Write Good Commit Messages" for more about this.

Finally, you should make it a habit to commit often. This will automatically help you to keep your commits small and only include related changes.

Inspecting the Commit History

Git saves every commit that is ever made in the course of your project. Especially when collaborating with others, it's important to see recent commits to understand what happened.

NOTE

Later in this book, in the Remote Repositories chapter, we'll talk about how to exchange data with your coworkers.

The "git log" command is used to display the project's commit history:

```
$ git log
```

It lists the commits in chronological order, beginning with the newest item. If there are more items than it can display on one page, the command line indicates this by showing a colon (":") at the end of the page. You can then go to the next page with the SPACE key and quit with the "q" key.

```
commit 2dfe283e6c81ca48d6edc1574b1f2d4d84ae7fa1
Author: Tobias Günther <support@learn-git.com>
Date: Fri Jul 26 10:52:04 2013 +0200

    Implement the new login box

commit 2b504bee4083a20e0ef1e037eea0bd913a4d56b6
Author: Tobias Günther <support@learn-git.com>
Date: Fri Jul 26 10:05:48 2013 +0200

    Change headlines for about and imprint

commit 0023cdddf42d916bd7e3d0a279c1f36bfc8a051b
Author: Tobias Günther <support@learn-git.com>
Date: Fri Jul 26 10:04:16 2013 +0200

    Add simple robots.txt
```

Every commit item consists (amongst other things) of the following metadata:

> Commit Hash
> Author Name & Email
> Date
> Commit Message

 GLOSSARY

The Commit Hash

Every commit has a unique identifier: a 40-character checksum called the "commit hash". While in centralized version control systems like Subversion or CVS, an ascending revision number is used for this, this is simply not possible anymore in a distributed VCS like Git: The reason herefore is that, in Git, multiple people can work in parallel, **commiting** their work **offline**, without being connected to a shared repository. In this scenario, you can't say anymore whose commit is #5 and whose is #6.

Since in most projects, the first 7 characters of the hash are enough for it to be unique, referring to a commit using a shortened version is very common.

Apart from this metadata, Git also allows you to display the detailed changes that happened in each commit. Use the "-p" flag with the "git log" command to add this kind of information:

```
$ git log -p
commit 2dfe283e6c81ca48d6edc1574b1f2d4d84ae7fa1
Author: Tobias Günther <support@learn-git.com>
Date: Fri Jul 26 10:52:04 2013 +0200

      Implement the new login box

diff --git a/css/about.css b/css/about.css
index e69de29..4b5800f 100644
--- a/css/about.css
+++ b/css/about.css
@@ -0,0 +1,2 @@
+h1 {
+   line-height:30px; }
\ No newline at end of file
di.ff --git a/css/general.css b/css/general.css
index a3b8935..d472b7f 100644
--- a/css/general.css
+++ b/css/general.css
@@ -21,7 +21,8 @@ body {

 h1, h2, h3, h4, h5 {
    color:#ffd84c;
-   font-family: "Trebuchet MS", "Trebuchet"; }
+   font-family: "Trebuchet MS", "Trebuchet";
+   margin-bottom:0px; }

 p {
    margin-bottom:6px;}
diff --git a/error.html b/error.html
deleted file mode 100644
index 78a1c33..0000000
--- a/error.html
+++ /dev/null
@@ -1,43 +0,0 @@
- <html>
-
-    <head>
-       <title>Tower :: Imprint</title>
-       <link rel="shortcut icon" href="img/favicon.ico" />
-       <link type="text/css" href="css/general.css" />
-    </head>
-
```

Later in this book, we'll learn how to interpret this kind of output in the chapter Inspecting Changes in Detail with Diffs.

Time to Celebrate

Congratulations! You've just taken the first step in mastering version control with Git! Pat yourself on the back and grab a beer before moving on.

CHAPTER 2:

BRANCHING &
MERGING

Branching can Change Your Life

This is quite a sensational headline, I know… But the truth is: it's not an exaggeration. Using branches in your day-to-day work might very well prove to make you a better programmer or designer.

First of all, if you're coming from another version control system, I kindly ask you to forget the things you already know about branching & merging. It's true that Git hasn't invented this particular wheel: many other VCS also offer branching. However, Git's concepts in this area are absolutely unique when it comes to ease of use and performance.

Now, let's look at why branches are so important.

Working in Contexts

In every project, there are always multiple different **contexts** where work happens. Each feature, bugfix, experiment, or alternative of your product is actually a context of its own: it can be seen as its own "topic", clearly separated from other topics.

This leaves you with an unlimited amount of different contexts. Most likely, you'll have at least one context for your "main" or "production" state, and another context for each feature, bugfix, experiment, etc.

In real-world projects, work always happens in multiple of these contexts in **parallel**:

› While you're preparing two new variations of your website's design (context 1 & 2)...

› you're also trying to fix an annoying bug (context 3).

› On the side, you also update some content on your FAQ pages (context 4), while...

› one of your teammates is working on a new feature for your shopping cart (context 5),...

› and another colleague is experimenting with a whole new login functionality (context 6).

A World Without Branches

Not working in clearly separated contexts can (and sooner or later **will**) cause several problems:

> What happens if your client likes variation 2 of the new design? In the meantime, a host of other changes have happened! How do you launch the new design while integrating all these other changes instead of losing them?

> What happens if the shopping cart feature became obsolete because the client changed his mind? How do you get all that unwanted code (and only that code!) out?

> What do you do if that new login functionality proves to be impossible to implement? It's already mingled with all of those other changes, being almost impossible to separate out!

> How can you avoid losing track? Most likely, you shouldn't be bothered with all the topics from all of your colleagues.

Things will start to get very confusing when you try to handle multiple topics in a single context:

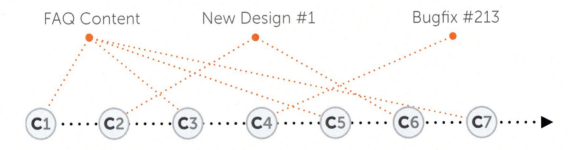

A tempting workaround might be to simply copy your complete project folder for each new context. But this only leaves you with other problems:

> You circumvent your VCS, since those new folders won't be under version control.

> Not being version controlled, you can't easily share & collaborate with others.

> Integrating changes from one context into another (maybe your main con-
text) is difficult and error-prone.

To make a long story short: if your goal is to work professionally, you'll have
to find a way to deal with multiple contexts in a professional manner.

Branches to the Rescue

You might have already guessed it: branches are what we need to solve these
problems. Because a branch represents exactly such a context in a project
and helps you keep it separate from all other contexts.

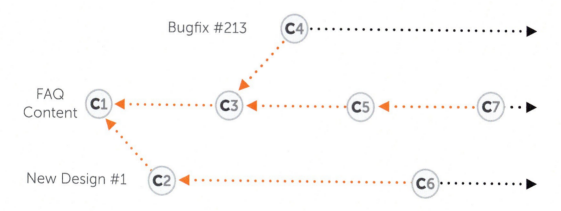

All the changes you make at any time will only apply to the **currently active**
branch; all other branches are left untouched. This gives you the freedom to
both work on different things in parallel and, above all, to experiment - because you can't mess up! In case things go wrong you can always go back /
undo / start fresh / switch contexts...

Luckily, branches in Git are cheap & easy. There's no reason not to create a new branch when you start working on a new topic, no matter how big or small it might be.

 THE GOLDEN RULES OF VERSION CONTROL

#3 Use Branches Extensively

Branching is one of Git's most powerful features — and this is not by accident: quick and easy branching was a central requirement from day one. Branches are the perfect tool to help you avoid mixing up different lines of development. You should use branches extensively in your development workflows: for new features, bug fixes, experiments, ideas...

Working with Branches

Until now, we haven't taken much notice of branches in our example project. However, without knowing, we were already working on a branch! This is because branches aren't optional in Git: you are **always** working on a certain branch (the currently **active**, or "**checked out**", or "**HEAD**" branch).

So, which branch is HEAD at the moment? The "git status" command tells us in its first line of output: "On branch master".

The "master" branch was created by Git automatically for us when we started the project. Although you could rename or delete it, you'll have a hard time finding a project without it because most people just keep it. But please keep in mind that "master" is by no means a special or magical branch. It's like any other branch!

Now, let's start working on a new feature. Based on the project's current state, we create a new branch and name it "contact-form":

```
$ git branch contact-form
```

Using the "git branch" command lists all of our branches (and the "-v" flag provides us with a little more data than usual):

```
$ git branch -v
  contact-form 3de33cc Implement the new login box
* master       3de33cc [ahead 1] Implement the new login box
```

You can see that our new branch "contact-form" was created and is based on the same version as "master". Additionally, the little asterisk character (*) next to "master" indicates that this is our current HEAD branch. To emphasize this: the "git branch" command only **created** that new branch - but it **didn't make**

it active. Before checking out that new branch, it's a good idea to have another look at "git status" to see where we currently are:

```
$ git status
# On branch master
# Changes not staged for commit:
#   (use "git add <file>..." to update what will be committed)
#   (use "git checkout -- <file>..." to discard changes in working
#   directory)
#
#       modified:    imprint.html
#
no changes added to commit (use "git add" and/or "git commit -a")
```

Oh, right: we still have some changes in "imprint.html" in our working copy! Actually, we just wanted to start working on our new "contact-form" branch; but these changes don't belong to this feature. So what do we do with them? One way to get this work-in-progress out of the way would be to simply commit it. But committing half-done work is a bad habit.

 The Golden Rules of Version Control:

#4: Never Commit Half-Done Work

You should only commit code when it's completed. This doesn't mean you have to complete a whole, large feature before committing. Quite the contrary: split the feature's implementation into logical chunks and remember to commit early and often. But don't commit just to get half-done work out of your way when you need a "clean working copy". For these cases, consider using Git's "Stash" feature instead.

Saving Changes Temporarily

A commit wraps up changes and saves them **permanently** in the repository. However, in your day-to-day work, there are a lot of situations where you only want to save your local changes **temporarily**. For example, imagine you're in the middle of some changes for feature X when an important bug report comes in. Your local changes don't belong to the bugfix you're going to make. You have to get rid of them (temporarily, without losing them!) and continue working on them later.

Situations like this one happen all the time: you have some local changes in your working copy that you can't commit right now - and you want or need to start working on something else. To get these changes out of your way and have a "clean" working copy, Git's "Stash" feature comes in handy.

CONCEPT

The Stash

Think of the Stash as a clipboard on steroids: it takes all the changes in your working copy and saves them for you on a new clipboard. You're left with a clean working copy, i.e. you have no more local changes.

Later, at any time, you can restore the changes from that clipboard in your working copy - and continue working where you left off.

You can create as many Stashes as you want - you're not limited to storing only one set of changes. Also, a Stash is not bound to the branch where you created it: when you restore it, the changes will be applied to your current HEAD branch, whichever this may be.

Let's stash away these local changes so we have a clean working copy before starting to work on our new feature:

```
$ git stash
Saved working directory and index state WIP on master:
    2dfe283 Implement the new login box
HEAD is now at 2dfe283 Implement the new login box
```

```
$ git status
# On branch master
nothing to commit (working directory clean)
```

The local changes in "imprint.html" are now safely stored on a clipboard, ready to be restored any time we want to continue working on them.

You can easily get an overview of your current Stashes:

```
$ git stash list
stash@{0}: WIP on master: 2d6e283 Implement the new login box
```

The newest Stash will always be at the top of the list, named "stash@{0}". Older Stashes have higher numbers.

When you're ready to restore a saved Stash, you have two options:

› Calling "git stash pop" will apply the newest Stash **and** clear it from your Stash clipboard.

› Calling "git stash apply <stashname>" will also apply the specified Stash, but it will **remain saved**. You can delete it later via "git stash drop <stashname>".

You can choose to **not** specify the Stash when using any of these commands. Then, Git will simply take the newest Stash (always "stash@{0}").

CONCEPT

When to Stash

Stashing helps you get a clean working copy. While this can be helpful in many situations, it's strongly recommended...

> ...before checking out a different branch.

> ...before pulling remote changes.

> ...before merging or rebasing a branch.

Finally, it's time to get our hands dirty with our new feature!

Checking Out a Local Branch

Now that we have a clean working copy, the first thing we have to do is switch to (or "check out") our newly created branch:

```
$ git checkout contact-form
```

 CONCEPT

Checkout, HEAD, and Your Working Copy

A branch automatically points to the latest commit in that context. And since a commit references a certain version of your project, Git always knows exactly which files belong to that branch.

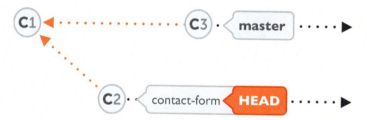

At each point in time, only **one** branch can be HEAD / checked out / active. The files in your working copy are those that are associated with this exact branch. All other branches (and their associated files) are safely stored in Git's database. To make another branch (say, "contact-form") active, the "git checkout" command is used. This does two things for you:

› It makes "contact-form" the current HEAD branch.

› It replaces the files in your working directory to match exactly the revision that "contact-form" is at.

Running "git status" once more, you'll see that we're now "On branch contact-form". From now on, all of our changes and commits will only impact
this very context - until we switch it again by using the "checkout" command
to make a different branch active.

Let's prove this by creating a new file called "contact.html" and committing it:

```
$ git add contact.html
$ git commit -m "Add new contact form page"
$ git log
commit 56eddd14cf034f4bcb8dc9cbf847b33309fa5180
Author: Tobias Günther <support@learn-git.com>
Date: Fri Jul 26 10:56:16 2013 +0200

    Add new contact form page

commit 2dfe283e6c81ca48d6edc1574b1f2d4d84ae7f1
Author: Tobias Günther <support@learn-git.com>
Date: Fri Jul 26 10:52:04 2013 +0200

    Implement the new login box

commit 2b504bee4083a20e0ef1e037eea0bd913a4d56b6
Author: Tobias Günther <support@learn-git.com>
Date: Fri Jul 26 10:05:48 2013 +0200

    Change headlines for about and imprint
```

Looking at the Log, you'll see that your new commit was properly saved. No
big surprises, so far. But now let's switch back to "master" and have a look at
the Log once more:

```
$ git checkout master
$ git log
commit 2dfe283e6c81ca48d6edc1574b1f2d4d84ae7f1
Author: Tobias Günther <support@learn-git.com>
Date: Fri Jul 26 10:52:04 2013 +0200

    Implement the new login box

commit 2b504bee4083a20e0ef1e037eea0bd913a4d56b6
Author: Tobias Günther <support@learn-git.com>
Date: Fri Jul 26 10:05:48 2013 +0200

    Change headlines for about and imprint
```

You'll find that the "Add new contact form page" commit isn't there - because we made it in the context of our HEAD branch (which was the "contact-form" branch, not the "master" branch). This is exactly what we wanted: our changes are kept in their own context, separated from other contexts.

Merging Changes

Keeping your commits in the separate context of a branch is a huge help. But there will come a time when you want to integrate changes from one branch into another. For example when you finished developing a feature and want to integrate it into your "production" branch. Or maybe the other way around: you're **not yet** finished working on your feature, but so many things have happened in the rest of the project in the meantime that you want to integrate these back into your feature branch.

Whatever the scenario may be: such an integration is called "merging" and is done with the "git merge" command.

CONCEPT

Integrating Branches - Not Individual Commits

When starting a merge, you don't have to (and cannot) pick **individual commits** that shall be integrated. Instead, you tell Git which **branch** you want to integrate - and Git will figure out which commits you don't have in your current working branch. Only these commits will then be integrated as a result.

Also, you never have to think long and hard about where these changes end up: The target of such an integration is always your current HEAD branch and, thereby, your working copy.

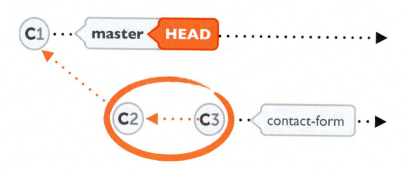

In Git, performing a merge is easy as pie. It requires just two steps:

1. Check out the branch that ha receive the changes.

2. Call the "git merge" command with the name of the branch that contains the desired changes.

Let's integrate the changes from our "contact-form" branch into "master":

```
$ git checkout master
$ git merge contact-form
```

When you now perform a "git log" command, you'll see that our "Add new contact form page" commit was successfully integrated into master!

```
$ git log
commit 56eddd14cf034f4bcb8dc9cbf847b33309fa5180
Author: Tobias Günther <support@learn-git.com>
Date: Fri Jul 26 10:56:16 2013 +0200

    Add new contact form page

commit 2dfe283e6c81ca48d6edc1574b1f2d4d84ae7f1
Author: Tobias Günther <support@learn-git.com>
Date: Fri Jul 26 10:52:04 2013 +0200

    Implement the new login box

commit 2b504bee4083a20e0ef1e037eea0bd913a4d56b6
Author: Tobias Günther <support@learn-git.com>
Date: Fri Jul 26 10:05:48 2013 +0200

    Change headlines for about and imprin
```

However, the result of a merge action can't always be displayed **that** clearly: not always can Git simply add the missing commits on top of the HEAD branch. Often, it will have to combine changes in a new, separate commit called a "merge commit". Think of it like a knot that connects two branches.

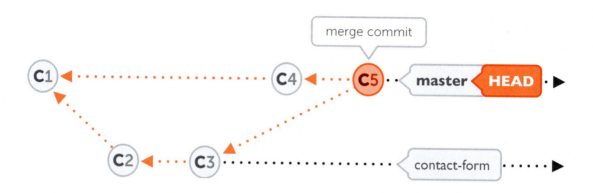

You can merge one branch into another as often as you like. Git will again figure out which changes haven't been merged and only consider these.

 CROSS REFERENCE

In some situations, merging will result in one or more "merge conflicts". In such a case, Git wasn't able to combine changes, e.g. because the exact same line was modified in two different ways. You'll then have to decide yourself which content you want. We'll talk about Dealing with Merge Conflicts in detail later in this book.

Branching Workflows

Depending on how they're used, you can divide branches into two major groups.

 NOTE
Please keep in mind, though, that this is just a semantic division. Technically (and practically), a branch is just a branch and always works in the same way.

(A) Short-Lived / Topic Branches

Earlier in this book, you've already read my advice to be generous about creating branches for **new features, bug fixes, and experiments**. Branches for these kinds of things share two important characteristics:

› They are about a **single topic** and are used to isolate code belonging to this topic from any other code. You shouldn't create a "shopping-cart" branch to then also commit code dealing with newsletter signup or bug #341 to it.

› They typically have a rather **short lifespan**, usually only until you've finished working on the topic (i.e. when the bug is fixed, the feature is complete...). Then, the branch will be integrated into the broader context of your project and can be deleted.

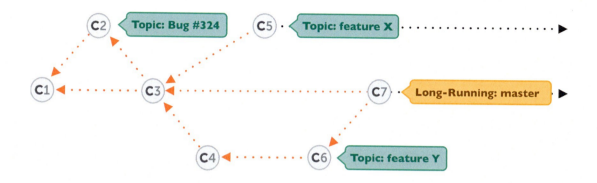

(B) Long-Running Branches

Other branches are used on a higher level, independent of a single feature or bugfix development. They represent states in your project lifecycle - like a "production", "testing", or "development" state - and remain in your project for a longer time (or even all the time). Typically, a couple of rules apply to this kind of branches:

› You shouldn't work on them directly. Instead, you **integrate other branches** (possibly feature branches or other long-running branches) into them, but rarely add commits directly to them.

› Often, long-running branches have a **hierarchy** between them: e.g. "master" is used as the highest-order branch. It should only contain production code. Subordinate to it exists a "development" branch. It's used to test developed features and is then integrated into "master"...

Which long-running branches should be created and how they should be used can't be generalized. This depends a lot on the team (its size and style of development) and the requirements of the project (and possibly also the customer). Clear rules must exist and be agreed on by everybody in the team.

A Very Simple Branching Strategy

As already said, each team must find its own branching strategy. However, we'll look at a very simple workflow that should fit for a lot of teams.

One Long-Running Branch Only

Although you could of course introduce multiple long-running branches, there are a couple of reasons against this: most notably, it complicates things! Having only a single long-running branch in your workflow keeps things as simple as possible.

 CONCEPT

In such a scenario, the "master" branch effectively represents your production code. This has one important consequence: **everything that gets merged into "master" must be stable!** It must be tested, reviewed, and approved by whatever methods else you have to assure quality.

This also means that no work should happen directly on "master" (which is also a very common rule). Therefore, if you should find yourself typing "git checkout master", followed by "git commit", you should ask yourself if you're doing the right thing...

Topic Branches

Every time you start working on a new feature or bugfix, you should create a new branch for this topic. This is a common practice in almost all branching work-flows and should become a habit for you, too.

As you only have a single long-running branch in your repository, all new topic branches are based off of this "master" branch. And when your work is done in this topic, of course, it should be merged back into "master".

In the meantime, it might be that new code gets integrated into "master" by your teammates while you're still working on your feature. It's both recom-mended and simple to merge new stuff often from master into your devel-opment branch. This ensures that you're staying up-to-date - and thereby reduces the risk of merge conflicts that come with large integrations.

Don't forget the golden rule that comes with such a simple workflow: code that gets integrated into "master" must be stable! How you ensure this is up to you and your team: use unit tests, code reviews, etc.

Keep the Remote in Sync

In Git, remote and local branches can be completely independent from each other. However, it makes great sense to regard local and remote branches as counterparts of each other.

This doesn't mean that you need to publish *each* of your local branches: it can still make perfect sense to keep some of your branches private, e.g. when you're doing experimental stuff that you're working on alone.

However, if you *do* publish a local branch, you should name its remote counterpart branch the same. If you have a local branch named "login-ui", you should also name it "login-ui" when you push it to your remote repository.

Push Often

Keeping the remote in sync doesn't stop with the structure: publishing your work often via "git push" makes sure that everybody has always access to the latest developments. And, as a bonus, it can serve as your remote backup.

Other Branching Strategies

The above strategy is best suited for small, agile teams. Especially larger teams might need more rules and more structures.

Searching the web for other teams' strategies will present you with many interesting alternatives. See our chapter on Workflows with git-flow for information on the popular **git-flow** workflow

 NOTE

In my personal opinion, git-flow is a bit too heavy of a component:

> It comes with its own script that introduces a layer on top of Git and its commands. This makes it hard to use from a GUI application.

> It comes with the noble endeavour to simplify Git - however, it thereby forces the user to learn almost a meta-language with new commands.

In my opinion, properly learning the Git basics and agreeing on a common workflow in a team makes "supplements" like git-flow superfluous.

## CHAPTER 3

REMOTE REPOSITORIES

About Remote Repositories

About 90% of version control related work happens in the local repository: staging, committing, viewing the status or the log/history, etc. Moreover, if you're the only person working on your project, chances are you'll never need to set up a remote repository.

Only when it comes to **sharing data** with your teammates, a remote repo comes into play. Think of it like a "file server" that you use to exchange data with your colleagues.

Let's look at the few things that distinguish local and remote repositories from each other:

Location

Local repositories reside on the computers of team members. In contrast, remote repositories are hosted on a server that is accessible for all team members - most likely on the internet or on a local network.

Features

Technically, a remote repository doesn't differ from a local one: it contains branches, commits, and tags just like a local repository. However, a local repository has a working copy associated with it: a directory where some version of your project's files is checked out for you to work with.

A remote repository doesn't have such a working directory: it only consists of the bare ".git" repository folder.

Creation

You have two options to get a local repository onto your machine: you can either create a new, empty one or clone it from an existing remote repository.

Creating a remote repository can also be done in two ways: if you already have a local repository that you want to base it on, you can clone this local one with the "--bare" option. In case you want to create a blank remote repository, use "git init", also with the "--bare" option.

Local / Remote Workflow

In Git, there are only a mere handful of commands that interact with a remote repository.

The overwhelming majority of work happens in the local repository. Until this point (except when we called "git clone"), we've worked exclusively with our local Git repository and never left our local computer. We were not dependent on any internet or network connection but instead worked completely offline. We'll look at each of these commands in the course of the following sections.

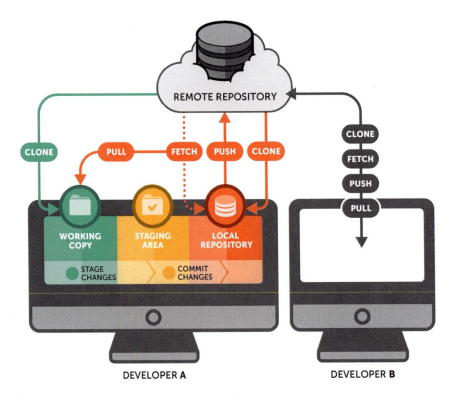

Connecting a Remote Repository

When you clone a repository from a remote server, Git automatically remembers this connection for you. It saves it as a remote called "origin" by default.

In other cases where you started with a fresh local repository, no remote connections are saved. In that situation, we need to connect our local repository to a new remote before we can try some remote interactions:

```
$ git remote add crash-course-remote
    https://github.com/gittower/git-crash-course-remote.git
```

Let's check if this worked out ok:

```
$ git remote -v
crash-course-remote     https://github.com/gittower/git-crash-course-remote.
git (fetch)
crash-course-remote     https://github.com/gittower/git-crash-course-remote.
git (push)
origin    https://github.com/gittower/git-crash-course (fetch)
origin    https://github.com/gittower/git-crash-course (push)
```

Note that each remote repository consists of two lines: the first one is the "fetch URL" which is used for reading access. The second one is the "push URL", used when you want to write data to the remote. In many cases, both URLs are the same. However, you can also use this to define different URLs for read and write access (for security and performance reasons).

Also note that you can connect as many remotes to a local repository as you like. In my case, you saw that another remote named "origin" is already present - although we didn't configure this! This was added by Git automatically when we cloned from the remote server (which we did at the beginning of this book). Exactly as with the "master" branch, the name "origin" for this remote is only a naming convention. It's just a normal remote repository like any other.

Inspecting Remote Data

So, what exactly did we achieve by connecting this new remote? Let's look at the list of branches:

```
$ git branch -va
  contact-form            56eddd1 Add new contact form page
* master                  56eddd1 Add new contact form page
  remotes/origin/HEAD     -> origin/master
  remotes/origin/master   2b504be Change headlines for about and imprint
```

Well, apparently not much happened: still our two local branches ("master" and "contact-form") and two items from our "origin" remote ("remotes/origin/HEAD" and "remotes/origin/master"). So why don't we see any data from our new "crash-course-remote"? Because, with the "git remote add" command, we have only established a relationship - but no data was exchanged so far.

 CONCEPT

Remote Data is a Snapshot

Git stores information about remote data (like branches, commits, etc.) in your local repository for you. However, there is no "live" connection to your remote. E.g. you will not automatically see new commits or branches that your teammates published on a remote.

The information about remote branches, remote commits, etc. is only as fresh as the last snapshot that you requested. There is no "automatic" update in the background.

To update the information about a remote, you have to explicitly request this data. Most notably, a "Fetch" operation does this for you:

```
$ git fetch crash-course-remote
From https://github.com/gittower/git-crash-course-remote
 * [new branch]      faq-content -> crash-course-remote/faq-content
 * [new branch]      master -> crash-course-remote/master
```

Fetch will not touch any of your local branches or the files in your working copy. It just downloads data from the specified remote and makes it visible for you. You can decide later if you want to integrate new changes into your local project.

After updating our information about the "crash-course-remote", let's take another look at the available branches:

```
$ git branch -va
  contact-form              56eddd1 Add new contact form page
* master                    56eddd1 Add new contact form page
  remotes/crash-course-remote/faq-content  e29fb3f Add FAQ questions
  remotes/crash-course-remote/master              2b504be Change headlines f...
  remotes/origin/HEAD       -> origin/master
  remotes/origin/master     2b504be Change headlines for about and imprint
```

Now we also get information about the branches on "crash-course-remote".

Let's start working on that "faq-content" branch. Currently, however, this is only a remote branch pointer. To be able to **work** with this branch - to have our working copy populated with its files - we need to create a new local branch that's based on this remote branch. We're telling the "git checkout" command which remote branch we want to have:

```
$ git checkout --track crash-course-remote/faq-content
Branch faq-content set up to track remote branch faq-content from crash-
course-remote.
Switched to a new branch 'faq-content'

$ git branch -va
  contact-form              56eddd1 Add new contact form page
* faq-content               e29fb3f Add FAQ questions
  master                    56eddd1 Add new contact form page
  remotes/crash-course-remote/faq-content  e29fb3f Add FAQ questions
  remotes/crash-course-remote/master       2b504be Change headlines f...
  remotes/origin/HEAD     -> origin/master
  remotes/origin/master   2b504be Change headlines for about and imprint
```

This command does a couple of things for us:

› It creates a new local branch with the same name as the remote one
  ("faq-content").

› It checks this new branch out, i.e. it makes it our local HEAD branch and
  populates our working copy with the associated files from that branch's latest
  revision.

› Since we're using the "--track" flag, it establishes a so-called "tracking relationship" between the new local branch and the remote branch it's based on.

CONCEPT

Tracking Branches

In general, branches have nothing to do with each other. However, a local branch can be set up to "track" a remote branch. Git will then inform you if one branch contains new commits that the other one doesn't have:

> If your local branch contains commits that haven't been published / pushed to the remote repository, your local branch is "**ahead**" of its remote counterpart branch by some commits.

> If your teammates, on their part, have uploaded commits to the remote, the remote branch will have commits that you haven't downloaded / pulled to your local branch, yet. Your local branch is then "**behind**" its remote counterpart branch.

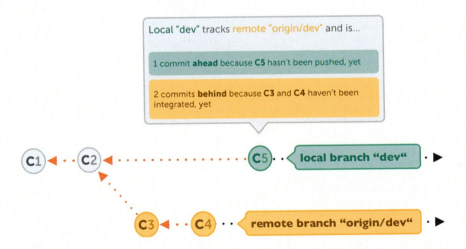

In case such a tracking relationship exists, Git will inform you about any discrepancies when performing "git status"

```
$ git status
# On branch dev
# Your branch and 'origin/dev' have diverged,
# and have 1 and 2 different commits each, respectively.
#
nothing to commit (working directory clean)
```

When creating a new local branch that is based on an existing remote branch, establishing a tracking connection is easy: simply use the
"git checkout" command with the "--track" flag set.

With a new local branch "faq-content" checked out, we're ready to contribute
to this feature. Let's make some modifications to the "faq.html" file that you now
have on your disk (I leave the details of these changes to your imagination...):

```
$ git status
# On branch faq-content
# Changes not staged for commit:
#   (use "git add <file>..." to update what will be committed)
#   (use "git checkout -- <file>..." to discard changes in working
#     directory)
#
#       modified:    faq.html
#
no changes added to commit (use "git add" and/or "git commit -a")

$ git add faq.html

$ git commit -m "Add new question"
[faq-content 814927a] Add new question
 1 file changed, 1 insertion(+)
```

Now it's time to share these brilliant changes we've just made with our colleagues:

```
$ git push
```

 NOTE

On your machine, this "git push" command will **not work** because you don't have write access to this remote repository. If you want to follow along and execute this command yourself, I recommend you create your own remote repository, for example on GitHub or Beanstalk.

The "git push" command uploads all the new commits from our current HEAD branch to its remote counterpart branch.

 CONCEPT

Tracking Connections Revisited

By default, the "git push" command expects us to provide it with two things:

> To which remote repository we want to push.

> To which branch on that remote repository we want to push.

The full command, therefore, looks something like this:

```
$ git push crash-course-remote faq-conten
```

With the tracking connection that we've set up already, we've defined a "remote counterpart" branch for our local branch. Git can then use this tracking information and lets us use the "git push" and "git pull" commands without further arguments.

Integrating Remote Changes

Sooner or later, one of your teammates will probably also share his changes on your common remote repository. Before integrating these changes into your local working copy, you might first want to inspect them:

```
$ git fetch origin
$ git log origin/master
```

 NOTE

Since you will most likely encounter an "origin" remote in most of your projects, we will use this remote name in our examples in the rest of the book.

The "git log" command now shows you the commits that happened recently on the "master" branch of the remote called "origin".

If you decide you want to integrate these changes into your working copy, the "git pull" command is what you need:

```
$ git pull
```

This command downloads new commits from the remote and directly integrates them into your working copy. It's actually a "fetch" command (which only downloads data) and a "merge" command (which integrates this data into your working copy) combined.

As with the "git push" command: in case no tracking connection was established for your local HEAD branch, you will also have to tell Git from which

Publishing a Local Branch

A local branch that you create on your machine is kept private to you until you explicitly decide to publish it. This means that it's perfectly possible to keep some of your work private while sharing only certain other branches with the world.

Let's share our "contact-form" branch (which hasn't been published until now) on the "origin" remote:

```
$ git checkout contact-form
Switched to branch 'contact-form'

$ git push -u origin contact-form
Counting objects: 36, done.
Delta compression using up to 4 threads.
Compressing objects: 100% (31/31), done.
Writing objects: 100% (36/36), 90.67 KiB, done.
Total 36 (delta 12), reused 0 (delta 0)
Unpacking objects: 100% (36/36), done.
To file://Users/tobidobi/Desktop/GitCrashkurs/remote-test.git
 * [new branch]    contact-form -> contact-form
Branch contact-form set up to track remote branch contact-form from ori-
gin.
```

This command tells Git to publish our current local HEAD branch on the "origin" remote under the name "contact-form" (it makes sense to keep names between local branches and their remote counterparts the same).

The "-u" flag establishes a tracking connection between that newly created branch on the remote and our local "contact-form" branch. Performing the "git branch" command with a special set of options also shows us the tracking relationships in square brackets:

```
$ git branch -vva
* contact-form                56eddd1 [origin/contact-form] Add new contact..
  faq-content                 814927a [crash-course-remote/faq-content: ahead
                                1] Add new question
  master                      2dfe283 Implement the new login box
  remotes/crash-course-remote/faq-content e29fb3f Add FAQ questions
  remotes/crash-course-remote/master      2b504be Change headlines f...
  remotes/origin/contact-form             56eddd1 Add new contact fo...
  remotes/origin/master  56eddd1 Add new contact form page
```

After having created that new remote branch like this, updating it with new local commits that you create in the future is easy: simply call the "git push" command with no options as we did in our earlier example.

Anyone with access to your remote repository can now also start working on "contact-form": he can create a local branch on his machine that tracks this remote branch and also push changes to it.

Deleting Branches

Let's assume our work on "contact-form" is done and we've already integrated it into "master". Since we don't need it anymore, we can delete it:

```
$ git branch -d contact-form
```

Tidy as we are, we also delete the remote branch by simply adding the „-r"
flag:

```
$ git branch -dr origin/contact-form
```

## CHAPTER 4

ADVANCED TOPICS

Undoing Things

One of the greatest aspects about Git is that you can undo almost anything. In the end, this means that you actually can't mess up: Git always provides a safety net for you.

Fixing the Last Commit

No matter how carefully you craft your commits, sooner or later you'll forget to add a change or mistype the commit's message. That's when the "--amend" flag of the "git commit" command comes in handy: it allows you to change the **very last** commit really easily.

If you just want to correct the commit message, you simply "commit again" - without any staged changes but **with** the correct message:

```
$ git commit --amend -m "This is the correct message"
```

In case you want to add some more changes to that last commit, you can simply stage them as normal and then commit again:

```
$ git add <some/changed/files>
$ git commit --amend -m "commit message
```

The Gold Rules of Version Control

#5: Never Amend Published Commits

Using the "amend" option is a great little helper that you'll come to appreciate yourself very quickly. However, you'll need to keep the following things in mind when using it:

› **(a)** It can only be used to fix the **very last** commit. Older commits can't be modified with "amend".

› **(b)** You should never "amend" a commit that has already been published / pushed to a remote repository! This is because "amend" effectively produces a completely new commit object in the background that replaces the old one. If you're the only person who had this commit, doing this is safe. However, after publishing the original commit on a remote, other people might already have based new work on this commit. Replacing it with an amended version will cause problems.

Undoing Local Changes

Changes are called "local" when they haven't been committed, yet: all the modifications that are currently present in your working directory are "local", uncommitted changes.

Sometimes, you'll produce code that... well... is worse than what you had before. These are the times when you want to discard these changes and start fresh with the last committed version.

To restore a file to its last committed version, you use the "git checkout" command:

```
$ git checkout HEAD file/to/restore.ext
```

You already know that the "checkout" command is mainly used to switch branches. However, if you use it with the HEAD reference and the path to a file, it will discard any uncommitted changes in that file.

If you need to discard **all** current changes in your working copy and want to restore the last committed version of your complete project, the "git reset" command is your friend:

```
$ git reset --hard HEAD
```

This tells Git to replace the files in your working copy with the "HEAD" revision (which is the last committed version), discarding all local changes.

NOTE

Discarding uncommitted changes cannot be undone. This is because they have never been saved in your repository. Therefore, Git has no chance to restore this kind of changes.

Always keep this in mind when discarding local changes.

Undoing Committed Changes

Sometimes you'll want to undo a certain commit. E.g. when you notice that your changes were wrong, when you introduced a bug, or simply when the customer has decided he doesn't want this anymore.

Using the "git revert" command is one possibility to undo a previous commit. However, the command doesn't **delete** any commits. Instead, it **reverts the effects** of a certain commit, effectively undoing it. It does this by producing a new commit with changes that revert each of the changes in that unwanted commit. For example, if your original commit added a word in a certain place, the reverting commit will remove exactly this word, again.

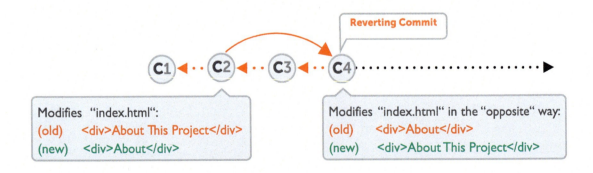

Simply provide the hash of the commit you want to revert:

```
$ git revert 2b504be
[master 364d412] Revert "Change headlines for about and imprint"
 2 files changed, 2 insertions(+), 2 deletions (-)

$ git log
commit 364d412a25ddce997ce76230598aaa7b9759f434
Author: Tobias Günther <support@learn-git.com>
Date: Tue Aug 6 10:23:57 2013 +0200

    Revert "Change headlines for about and imprint"

    This reverts commit 2b504bee4083a20e0ef1e037eea0bd913a4d56b6.
```

Another tool to "undo" commits is the "git reset" command. It neither pro-duces any new commits nor does it delete any old ones. It works by resetting your current HEAD branch to an older revision (also called "rolling back" to that older revision):

```
$ git reset --hard 2be18d9
```

After this command, your currently checked out branch will be at revision 2be18d9. The commits that came after this one are effectively undone and are no longer visible in the history of this branch.

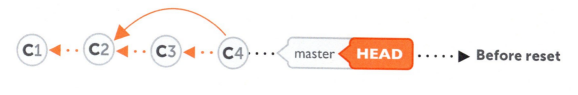

Be careful, however: calling the command with the "--hard" option will discard all local changes that you might currently have.
The project is completely restored as it was in that past revision.

If you call it with "--keep" instead of "--hard", all changes from rolled back revisions will be preserved as local changes in your working directory.

 NOTE

Just like "revert", the "reset" command also doesn't delete any commits. It just makes it look as if they hadn't existed and removes them from the history. However, they are still stored in Git's database for at least 30 days. So if you should ever notice you _accidentally_ removed commits you still need, one of your Git expert colleagues will still be able to restore them for you.

Both commands, revert and reset, only affect your current HEAD branch. Therefore, you should make sure you have checked out the correct branch before starting to play with them.

Inspecting Changes in Detail with Diffs

Driving a project forward requires a myriad of small changes. Understanding each of these individual changes is the key to understanding how the project evolved. While commands like "git status" or the plain "git log" command only inform you on a very broad level, there are other commands that display modifications in detail.

Reading Diffs

In version control, differences between two versions are presented in what's called a "diff" (or, synonymously, a "patch"). Let's take a detailed look at such a diff - and learn how to read it.

Compared Files a/b

Our diff compares two items with each other: item A and item B. In most cases, A and B will be the same file, but in different versions. Although not used very often, a diff could also compare two completely unrelated files with each other to show how they differ.

To make clear what is actually compared, a diff output always starts by declaring which files are represented by "A" and "B".

File Metadata

The file metadata shown here is a very technical information which you'll probably never need in practice. The first two numbers represent the hashes (or, simply put: "IDs") of our two files: Git saves every version not only of the project but also of each file as an object. Such a hash identifies a file object at a specific revision. The last number is an internal file mode identifier (100644 is just a "normal file", while 100755 specifies an executable file and 120000 represents a symbolic link).

Markers for a/b

Further down in the output, the actual changes will be marked as coming from A or B. In order to tell them apart, A and B are each assigned a symbol: for version A, this is a minus ("-") sign and for version B, a plus ("+") sign is used.

Chunk

A diff doesn't show the complete file from beginning to end: you wouldn't want to see everything in a 10,000 lines file, when only 2 lines have changed. Instead, it only shows those portions that were actually modified. Such a portion is called a "chunk" (or "hunk"). In addition to the actual changed lines, a chunk also contains a bit of "context": some (unchanged) lines before and after the modification so you can better understand in what context that change happened.

Chunk Header

Each of these chunks is prepended by a header. Enclosed in two "@" signs each, Git tells you which lines were affected. In our case the following lines are represented in the first chunk:

> From file A (represented by a "-"), 6 lines are extracted, beginning from line no. 34

> From file B (represented by a "+"), 8 lines are displayed, also starting from line no. 34

The text after the closing pair of "@@" aims to clarify the context, again: Git tries to display a method name or other contextual information of where this chunk was taken from in the file. However, this greatly depends on the programming language and doesn't work in all scenarios.

Changes

Each changed line is prepended with either a "+" or a "-" symbol. As explained, these symbols help you understand how exactly version A and B look: a line that is prepended with a "-" sign comes from A, while a line with a "+" sign comes from B.

In most cases, Git picks A and B in such a way that you can think of A/- as "old" content and B/+ as "new" content.

Let's look at our example:

> Change #1 contains two lines prepended with a "+". Since no counterpart in A existed for these lines (no lines with "-"), this means that these lines were added.

> Change #2 is just the opposite: in A, we have two lines marked with "-" signs. However, B doesn't have an equivalent (no "+" lines), meaning they were deleted.

> In change #3, finally, some lines were actually modified: the two "-" lines were changed to look like the two "+" lines below.

Now that we know how to read a diff output, let's generate some!

Inspecting Local Changes

Earlier in the book, we often used the "git status" command to see which files were currently changed in our working copy. To understand **how** they were changed in detail, we can ask "git diff":

```
$ git diff
diff --git a/about.html b/about.html
index d09ab79..0c20c33 100644
--- a/about.html
+++ b/about.html
@@ -19,7 +19,7 @@
     </div>

     <div id="headerContainer">
-       <h1>About</h1>
+       <h1>About This Project</h1>
     </div>

     <div id="contentContainer">
diff --git a/imprint.html b/imprint.html
index 1932d95..d34d56a 100644
--- a/imprint.html
+++ b/imprint.html
@@ -19,7 +19,7 @@
     </div>

     <div id="headerContainer">
-       <h1>Imprint</h1>
+       <h1>Imprint / Disclaimer</h1>
     </div>

     <div id="contentContainer">
```

Without further options, "git diff" will show us all current local changes in our working copy that are unstaged.

If you want to see only changes that have already been added to the Staging Area, "git diff --staged" is your command of choice.

Inspecting Committed Changes

You already know that the "git log" command provides you with an overview of recent commits. If you want to see more than the standard metadata (hash, author, date, message), then you can add the "-p" flag to get the detailed "patches" of each commit.

Comparing Branches & Revisions

Finally, you might want to know how one branch (or even a specific revision) differs from another one. Let's see all the changes from the "contact-form" branch that we don't have in "master", yet:

```
$ git diff master..contact-form
```

Instead of requesting such information on the branch level, you can even compare two arbitrary revisions with each other:

```
$ git diff 0023cdd..fcd6199
```

Dealing with Merge Conflicts

For a lot of people, merge conflicts are as scary as accidentally formatting their hard drive. In the course of this chapter, I want to relieve you from this fear.

You Cannot Break Things

The first thing that you should keep in mind is that you can always undo a merge and go back to the state before the conflict occurred. You're always able to undo and start fresh.

If you're coming from another version control system like e.g. Subversion you might be traumatized: conflicts in Subversion have the (rightful) reputation of being incredibly complex and nasty. One reason for this is that Git, simply stated, works completely different in this regard than Subversion. As a consequence, Git is able to take care of most things during a merge - leaving you with comparatively simple scenarios to solve.

Also, a conflict will only ever handicap yourself. It will **not** bring your complete team to a halt or cripple your central repository. This is because, in Git, conflicts can only occur on a developer's local machine - and not on the server.

How a Merge Conflict Occurs

In Git, "merging" is the act of integrating another branch into your current working branch. You're taking changes from another context (that's what a branch effectively is: a context) and combine them with your current working files. A great thing about having Git as your version control system is that it makes merging extremely easy: in most cases, Git will figure out how to integrate new changes.

However, there's a handful of situations where you might have to step in and tell Git what to do. Most notably, this is when changing the same file. Even in this case, Git will most likely be able to figure it out on its own. But if two people changed the same lines in that same file, or if one person decided to delete it while the other person decided to modify it, Git simply cannot know what is correct. Git will then mark the file as having a conflict - which you'll have to solve before you can continue your work.

How to Solve a Merge Conflicts

When faced with a merge conflict, the first step is to understand what happened. E.g.: Did one of your colleagues edit the same file on the same lines as you? Did he delete a file that you modified? Did you both add a file with the same name?

Git will tell you that you have "unmerged paths" (which is just another way of telling you that you have one or more conflicts) via "git status":

```
$ git status
# On branch contact-form
# You have unmerged paths.
#   (fix conflicts and run "git commit")
#
# Unmerged paths:
#   (use "git add <file>..." to mark resolution)
#
#        both modified:    contact.html
#
no changes added to commit (use "git add" and/or "git commit -a")
```

Let's take an in-depth look on how to solve the most common case, when two changes affected the same file on the same lines.

Now is the time to have a look at the contents of the conflicted file. Git was nice enough to mark the problematic area in the file by enclosing it in "<<<<<<< HEAD" and ">>>>>>> [other/branch/name]".

```
1    <<<<<<< HEAD
2    This line was committed while working in the "login-box" branch.
3    =======
4    This line, in contrast, was committed while working in the "contact-form" branch.
5    >>>>>>> refs/heads/contact-form
```

The contents after the first marker originate from your current working branch. After the angle brackets, Git tells us where (from which branch) the changes came from. A line with "=======" separates the two conflicting changes.

Our job is now to clean up these lines: when we're done, the file should look exactly as we want it to look. It can be necessary to consult the teammate who wrote the conflicting changes to decide which code is finally correct.

Maybe it's yours, maybe it's his - or maybe a mixture between the two.

Opening the raw file in your editor and cleaning it up there is perfectly valid, but not very comfortable. Using a dedicated merge tool can make this job a great deal easier (if you have one installed…). You can configure your tool of choice using the "git config" command. Consult your tool's documentation for detailed instructions.

Then, in case of a conflict, you can later invoke it by simply typing "git mergetool".

For this example, I've used "Kaleidoscope.app" on Mac:

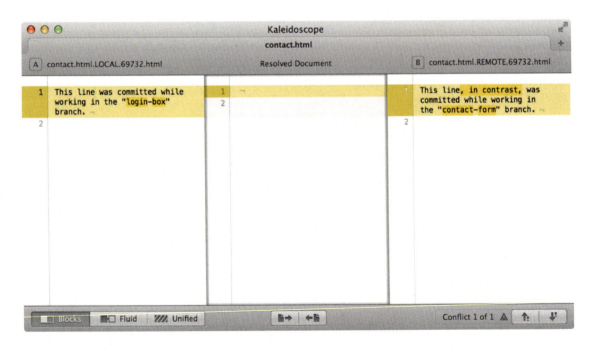

The left and right panes stand for the conflicting changes; a far more elegant visualization than "<<<<<<<" and ">>>>>>>". You can now simply toggle which change shall be taken. The middle pane shows the resulting code; in good tools, you can even edit this further.

Now, after cleaning up the file with the final code, all that's left is to save it. To give Git a hint that you're done with this file, you should quit the merge tool to continue. Behind the scenes, this told Git to execute a "git add" command on the (now formerly) conflicted file. This marks the conflict as solved. Should you decide _not_ to use a merge tool and instead clean up the file in your editor, you'll have to mark the file as resolved by hand (by executing "git add <filename>").

Finally, after solving all conflicts, a merge conflict situation needs to be concluded by a regular commit.

How to Undo a Merge

You should always keep in mind that you can return to the state before you started the merge at any time. This should give you the confidence that you can't break anything. On the command line, a simple "git merge --abort" will do this for you.

In case you've made a mistake while resolving a conflict and realize this only after completing the merge, you can still easily undo it: just roll back to the commit before the merge happened with "git reset --hard <commit-hash>" and start over again.

Rebase as an Alternative to Merge

While merging is definitely the easiest and most common way to integrate changes, it's not the only one: "Rebase" is an alternative means of integration.

> **NOTE**
>
> While rebasing definitely has its advantages over an off-the-shelf merge, it's also a matter of taste to a great extent: some teams prefer to use rebase, others prefer merge.
>
> As rebasing is quite a bit more complex than merging, my recommendation is that you skip this chapter unless you and your team are absolutely sure you want to use it. Another option is to return to this chapter after you've had some practice with the basic workflow in Git.

Understanding Merge a Little Better

Before we can dive into rebase, we'll have to get into a little more detail about merge. When Git performs a merge, it looks for three commits:

› **(1) Common ancestor commit**
  If you follow the history of two branches in a project, they always have at least one commit in common: at this point in time, both branches had the same content and then evolved differently.

› **(2) + (3) Endpoints of each branch**
  The goal of an integration is to combine the current states of two branches. Therefore, their respective latest revisions are of special interest.

Combining these three commits will result in the integration we're aiming for.

Fast-Forward or Merge Commit

In very simple cases, one of the two branches doesn't have any new commits since the branching happened - its latest commit is still the common ancestor.

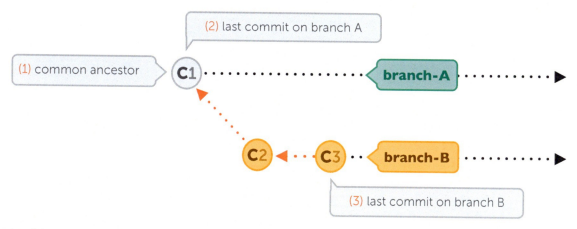

In this case, performing the integration is dead simple: Git can just add all the commits of the other branch on top of the common ancestor commit. In Git, this simplest form of integration is called a "fast-forward" merge. Both branches then share the exact same history.

In a lot of cases, however, both branches moved forward individually.

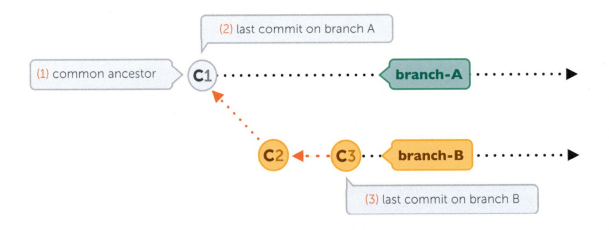

To make an integration, Git will have to create a new commit that contains the differences between them - the merge commit.

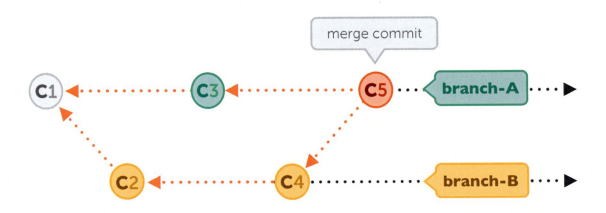

Human Commits & Merge Commits

Normally, a commit is carefully created by a human being. It's a meaningful unit that wraps only related changes and annotates them with a comment.

A merge commit is a bit different: instead of being created by a developer, it gets created *automatically* by Git. And instead of wrapping a set of related changes, its purpose is to connect two branches, just like a knot. If you want to understand a merge operation later, you need to take a look at the history of both branches and the corresponding commit graph.

Integrating with Rebase

Some people prefer to go without such automatic merge commits. Instead, they want the project's history to look as if it had evolved in a single, straight line. No indication remains that it had been split into multiple branches at some point.

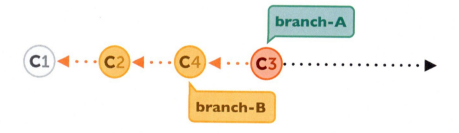

Let's walk through a rebase operation step by step. The scenario is the same as in the previous examples: we want to integrate the changes from branch-B into branch-A, but now by using rebase.

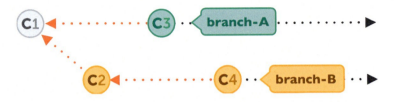

The command for this is very plain:

```
$ git rebase branch-B
```

First, Git will "undo" all commits on branch-A that happened after the lines began to branch out (after the common ancestor commit). However, of course, it won't discard them: instead you can think of those commits as being *"saved away temporarily"*.

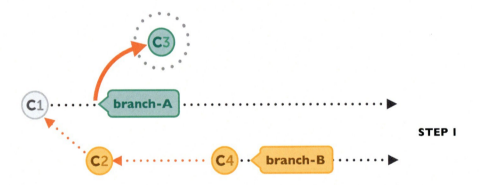

STEP 1

Next, it applies the commits from branch-B that we want to integrate. At this point, both branches look exactly the same.

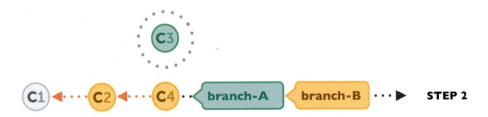

STEP 2

In the final step, the new commits on branch-A are now reapplied - but on a new position, on top of the integrated commits from branch-B (they are **rebased**).

The result looks like development had happened in a straight line. Instead of a merge commit that contains all the combined changes, the original commit structure was preserved.

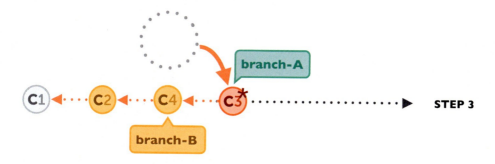

The Pitfalls of Rebase

Of course, using rebase isn't just sunshine and roses. You can easily shoot yourself in the foot if you don't mind an important fact: **rebase rewrites history**.

As you might have noticed in the last diagram above, commit "C3*" has an asterisk symbol added. This is because, although it has the same contents as "C3", it's effectively a different commit. The reason for this is that it now has a new parent commit (C4, which it was rebased onto, compared to C1, when it was originally created).

A commit has only a handful of important properties like the author, date, changeset - and who its parent commit is. Changing any of this information effectively creates a **new** commit, with a new hash ID.

Rewriting history in such a way is unproblematic as long as it only affects commits that haven't been published, yet. If instead you're rewriting commits that have already been pushed to a public server, danger is at hand: another developer has probably already based work on the original C3 commit, making it indispensable for other newer commits. Now you introduce the contents of C3 another time (with C3*), and additionally try to remove the original C3 from the timeline with your rebase. This smells like trouble...

Therefore, you should use rebase only for cleaning up your local work - but never to rebase commits that have already been published.

Submodules

Often in a project, you want to include libraries and other resources. The manual way is to simply download the necessary code files, copy them to your project, and commit the new files into your Git repository.

While this is a valid approach, it's not the cleanest one. By casually throwing those library files into your project, we're inviting a couple of problems:

› This mixes external code with our own, unique project files. The library, actually, is a project of itself and should be kept separate from our work. There's no need to keep these files in the same version control context as our project.

› Should the library change (because bugs were fixed or new features added), we'll have a hard time updating the library code. Again, we need to download the raw files and replace the original items.

Since these are quite common problems in everyday projects, Git of course offers a solution: Submodules.

Repositories Inside Repositories

A "Submodule" is just a standard Git repository. The only specialty is that it is nested inside a parent repository. In the common case of including a code library, you can simply add the library as a Submodule in your main project.

A Submodule remains a fully functional Git repository: you can modify files, commit, pull, push, etc. from inside it like with any other repository.

Let's see how to work with Submodules in practice.

Adding a Submodule

In our sample project, we create a new "lib" folder to host this (and future) library code.

```
$ mkdir lib
$ cd lib
```

With the "git submodule add" command, we'll add a little Javascript library from GitHub:

```
$ git submodule add https://github.com/djyde/ToProgress
```

Let's have a look at what just happened:

› (1) The command started a simple cloning process of the specified Git repository:

```
Cloning into 'lib/ToProgress'...
remote: Counting objects: 180, done.
remote: Compressing objects: 100% (89/89), done.
remote: Total 180 (delta 51), reused 0 (delta 0), pack-reused 91
Receiving objects: 100% (180/180), 29.99 KiB | 0 bytes/s, done.
Resolving deltas: 100% (90/90), done.
Checking connectivity... done.
```

› (2) Of course, this is reflected in our file structure: our project now contains
a new "ToProgess" folder inside the "lib" directory. As you can see from the
".git" subfolder contained herein, this is a fully-featured Git repository.

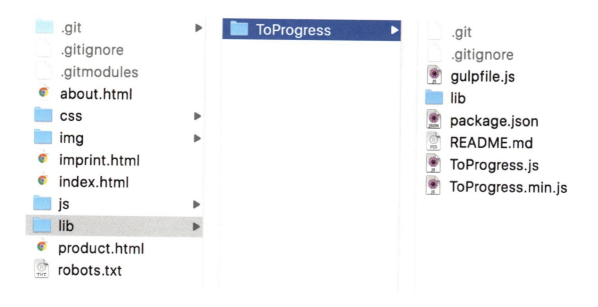

CONCEPT

It's important to understand that the actual contents of a Submodule are not stored in its parent repository. Only its remote URL, the local path inside the main project and the checked out revision are stored by the main repository.

Of course, the Submodule's working files are placed inside the specified directory in your project - in the end, you want to use the library's files! But they are not part of the parent project's version control contents.

› (3) A new ".gitmodules" file was created. This is where Git keeps track of our Submodules and their configuration:

```
[submodule "lib/ToProgress"]
    path = lib/ToProgress
    url = https://github.com/djyde/ToProgress
```

› (4) In case you're interested in the inner workings of Git: besides the ".git-modules" configuration file, Git also keeps record of the Submodule in your local ".git/config" file. Finally, it also keeps a copy of each Submodule's .git repository in its internal ".git/modules" folder.

 CONCEPT

Git's internal management of Submodules is quite complex (as you can already guess from all the .gitmodules, .git/config, and .git/modules entries...). Therefore, it's highly recommended not to mess with configuration files and values manually. Please do yourself a favor and always use proper Git commands to manage Submodules.

Let's have a look at our project's status:

```
$ git status
On branch master
Changes to be committed:
    (use "git reset HEAD ..." to unstage)

    new file:   .gitmodules
    new file:   lib/ToProgress
```

Git regards adding a Submodule as a modification like any other - and requests you to commit it to the repository:

```
$ git commit -m "Add 'ToProgress' Javascript library as Submodule"
```

Congratulations: we've now successfully added a Submodule to our main project! Before we look at a couple of use cases, let's see how you can clone a project that already *has* Submodules added.

Cloning a Project with Submodules

You already know that a project repository does *not* contain its Submodules' files; the parent repository only saves the Submodules' *configurations* as part of version control. This shows when you clone a project that contains Submodules: by default, the "git clone" command only downloads the project itself. Our "lib" folder, however, would stay empty.

You have two options to end up with a populated "lib" folder (or wherever else you choose to save your Submodules; "lib" is just an example):

› (a) You can add the "--recurse-submodules" option to "git clone"; this tells Git to also initialize all Submodules when the cloning is finished.

› (b) If you used a simple "git clone" command without this option, you need to initialize the Submodules afterwards with "git submodule update --init --recursive"

Checking Out a Revision

A Git repository can have countless committed versions, but only one version's files can be in your working directory. Therefore, like with any Git repository, you have to decide which revision of your Submodule shall be checked out.

 CONCEPT

Unlike normal Git repositories, Submodules always point to a specific commit - not a branch. This is because the contents of a branch can change over time, as new commits arrive. Pointing at a specific revision, on the other hand, guarantees that the correct code is always present.

Let's say we want to have an older version of our "ToProgress" library in our project. First, we'll have a look at the library's commit history. We change into the Submodule's base folder and call the "log" command:

```
$ cd lib/ToProgress/
$ git log --oneline --decorate
```

Before we take a look at the actual history, I'd like to stress an important point: Git commands are context-sensitive! By moving into the Submodule directory on the command line, all Git commands that we perform will be executed in the context of the Submodule, not its parent repository.

Now, in the log output, we spot a commit that is tagged "0.1.1":

```
83298f7 (HEAD, master) update .gitignore
a3b6186 remove page
ed693b7 update doc
3557a0e (tag: 0.1.1) change version code
2421796 update readme
```

This is the version we want to have in our project. To start with, we can simply check out this commit:

```
$ git checkout 0.1.1
```

Let's see what our parent repository thinks about all this. In the main project's base folder, execute:

```
$ git submodule status
+3557a0e0f7280fb3aba18fb9035d204c7de6344f   lib/ToProgress (0.1.1)
```

With "git submodule status", we're told which revision each Submodule is checked out at. The little "+" symbol in front of the hash is especially import-ant: it tells us that the Submodule is at a **different** revision than is officially recorded in the parent repository. This makes sense - since we just changed the checked out revision to the commit tagged "0.1.1".

When performing a simple "git status" in the parent repository, we see that Git regards moving the Submodule's pointer as a change like any other:

```
$ git status
On branch master
Changes not staged for commit:
    (use "git add ..." to update what will be committed)
    (use "git checkout -- ..." to discard changes in working directory)

    modified:    lib/ToProgress (new commits)
```

We need to commit this to the repository in order to make it official:

```
$ git commit -a -m "Moved Submodule pointer to version 1.1.0"
```

Updating a Submodule When its Pointer was Moved

We just saw how to check out a Submodule at a specific revision. But what if one of our teammates does this in our project? Let's say we integrate his changes (through pull, merge, or rebase for example) after he has moved the Submodule pointer to a different revision:

```
$ git pull
Updating 43d0c47..3919c52
Fast-forward
 lib/ToProgress | 2 +-
 1 file changed, 1 insertion(+), 1 deletion(-)
```

Git informs us, in a rather shy way, that "lib/ToProgress" was changed. Again, "git submodule status" provides more detailed information:

```
$ git submodule status
+83298f72c975c29f727c846579c297938492b245 lib/ToProgress (0.1.1-8-g83298f7)
```

Remember that little "+" sign? It tells us that the Submodule revision was moved - the version we currently have checked out in our project is not the one that is "officially" committed.

The "update" command helps us correct this:

```
$ git submodule update lib/ToProgress
Submodule path 'lib/ToProgress': checked out '3557a0e0f7280f-
b3aba18fb9035d204c7de6344f'
```

 NOTE

In most cases, you can use the „git submodule" family of commands without specifying a particular Submodule. By providing a path like in the example above, however, you can address just a certain Submodule.

We now have the same version of the Submodule checked out that our teammate had committed to the repository.

Note that the "update" command also downloads changes for you: imagine that your teammate moved the Submodule's pointer to a revision that you don't have, yet. In that case, Git fetches the corresponding revision in the Submodule and then checks it out for you. Very handy.

Checking for New Changes in the Submodule

Normally, you don't want library code to change very often: you'll want to use a version of the Submodule that you've tested and which you know works flawlessly with your own code. However, one of the best things about Submodules is that you can easily keep up with new releases (or minor new improvements).

Let's see if there's new code available in the Submodule:

```
$ cd lib/ToProgress
$ git fetch
remote: Counting objects: 3, done.
remote: Compressing objects: 100% (3/3), done.
remote: Total 3 (delta 0), reused 0 (delta 0), pack-reused 0
Unpacking objects: 100% (3/3), done.
From https://github.com/djyde/ToProgress
   83298f7..3e20bc2  master     -> origin/master
```

Note that, to do this, we simply change into the Submodule folder - and can then work like with any normal Git repository (because it is a normal Git repository).

The "git fetch" command, in this case, shows that there are indeed some new changes on the Submodule's remote.

CONCEPT

Before we go ahead and integrate these changes, I'd like to stress an important point once more. When checking the Submodule's status, we're informed that we're on a **detached HEAD**:

```
$ git status
    HEAD detached at 3557a0e
    nothing to commit, working directory clean
```

Normally, in Git, you always have a certain branch checked out. However, you can also choose to check out a specific **commit** (one that is **not** the tip of a branch). This is a rather rare case in Git and should normally be avoided.

However, when working with Submodules, it is the normal state to have a certain commit (and not a branch) checked out. You want to make sure you have an exact, static commit checked out in your project - not a branch which, by its nature, moves on with newer commits.

Now, let's integrate the new changes by pulling them into our local Submodule repository. Note that you cannot use the shorthand "git pull" syntax but instead need to specify the remote and branch, too.

This is because of the "detached HEAD" state we're in: since you're not a local branch at the moment, you need to tell Git on which branch you want to integrate the pulled down changes.

```
$ git pull origin master
```

If you now were to execute "git status" once more, you'd notice that we're still on that same detached HEAD commit as before - the currently checked out commit was not moved like when we're on a branch. If we want to use the new Submodule code in our main project, we have to explicitly move the HEAD pointer:

```
$ git checkout master
```

We're done working in our Submodule; let's move back into our main project:

```
$ cd ../..
$ git submodule status
+3e20bc25457aa56bdb243c0e5c77549ea0a6a927 lib/ToProgress (0.1.1-9-g3e20bc2)
```

Since we've just moved the Submodule pointer to a different revision, we need to commit this change to the main repository to make it official.

Working in a Submodule

In some cases, you might want to make some custom changes to a Submodule. You've already seen that working in a Submodule is like working in any other Git repository: any Git commands that you perform inside a Submodule directory are executed in the context of that sub-repository.

Let's say you want to change a tiny bit in a Submodule; you make your changes in the corresponding files, add them to the staging area and commit them.

This *might* already be the first banana skin: you should make sure you currently have a *branch* checked out in the Submodule before you commit. That's because if you're in a detached HEAD situation, your commit will easily get lost: it's not attached to any branch and will be gone as soon as you check out anything else.

Apart from that, everything else you've already learned still applies: in the main project, "git submodule status" will tell you that the Submodule pointer was moved and that you'll have to commit the move.

By the way: In case you have *uncommitted* local changes inside the Submodule, Git will also tell you in the main project:

```
$ git status
...
    modified:    lib/ToProgress (modified content)
```

Make sure to always keep a clean state in your Submodules.

Deleting a Submodule

Rather seldomly will you want to remove a Submodule from your project. But if you really want to do this, please don't do this manually: trying to mess with all the configuration files in a correct way will almost inevitably cause problems.

```
$ git submodule deinit lib/ToProgress
$ git rm lib/ToPogress
$ git status
...
    modified:    .gitmodules
    deleted:    lib/ToProgress
```

With "git submodule deinit", we made sure that the Submodule is cleanly re-moved from the configuration files.

With "git rm", we finally delete the actual Submodule files - and other obso-lete parts of your configuration.

Commit this and your Submodule will be cleanly removed from the project.

Workflows with git-flow

When using version control in a team, it's crucial to agree on a workflow. Git in particular allows to do lots of things in lots of ways. However, if you don't use a common workflow in your team, confusion is inevitable.

In principle, you're free to define your workflow of choice just as you want it - or you simply adopt an *existing* one.

In this chapter, we'll look at a workflow that has become quite popular in recent years: "git-flow".

What is git-flow?

By installing git-flow, you'll have a handful of extra commands available. Each of these commands performs multiple tasks automatically and in a predefined order. And voila - there we have our workflows!

git-flow is by no means a replacement for Git. It's just a set of scripts that combine standard Git commands in a clever way.

Strictly speaking, you wouldn't even have to install anything to use the git-flow workflows: you could easily learn which workflow involves which individual tasks - and simply perform these Git commands (with the right parameters and in the right order) on your own. The git-flow scripts, however, save you from having to memorize all of this.

Installing git-flow

A couple of different forks of git-flow have emerged in recent years. In this chapter, we're using one of the most popular ones: the AVH Edition.

For details on how to install git-flow, please have a look at the official documentation.

Setting Up git-flow in a Project

When you "switch on" git-flow in a project, Git still works the same way in this repository. It is totally up to you to use special git-flow commands and normal Git commands in this repository side by side. Put another way, git-flow doesn't *alter* your repository in any dramatic way.

That being said, however, git-flow indeed expects some conventions. Let's initialize it in a new project and we'll instantly see:

```
$ git flow init
Initialized empty Git repository in /Users/tobi/acme-website/.git/
Branch name for production releases: [master]
Branch name for "next release" development: [develop]

How to name your supporting branch prefixes?
Feature branches? [feature/]
Release branches? [release/]
Hotfix branches? [hotfix/]
```

When calling "git flow init" in the base folder of a project (no matter if it already *contains* an existing Git repository or not), an interactive setup assistant guides you through the initialization. This sounds a bit pompous... because actually, it's just about configuring some naming conventions for your branches.

Although the setup assistant allows you to enter any names you like, I strongly suggest you stick with the default naming scheme and simply confirm each step.

Branching Model

The git-flow model expects two main branches in a repository:

› **master** always and exclusively contains production code. You don't work directly on the master branch but instead in designated, separate feature branches (which we'll talk about in a minute). Not committing directly to the master branch is a common hygiene rule in many workflows.

> **develop** is the basis for any new development efforts you make: when you start a new feature branch it will be based on develop. Additionally, this branch also aggregates any finished features, waiting to be integrated and deployed via *master*.

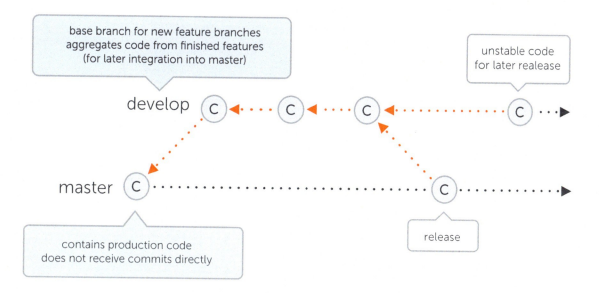

These two branches are so-called Branching Workflows branches: they remain in your project during its whole lifetime. Other branches, e.g. for features or releases, only exist temporarily: they are created on demand and are deleted after they've fulfilled their purpose.

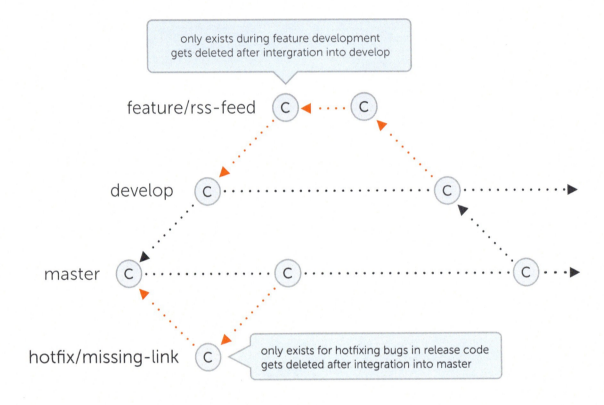

Let's start exploring all of this in some real-world use cases.

Feature Development

Working on a feature is by far the most common task for any developer. That's why git-flow offers a couple of workflows around feature development that help do this in an organized way.

Starting a New Feature

Let's start working on a new "rss-feed" feature:

```
$ git flow feature start rss-feed
Switched to a new branch 'feature/rss-feed'

Summary of actions:
- A new branch 'feature/rss-feed' was created, based on 'develop'
- You are now on branch 'feature/rss-feed'
```

 CONCEPT

At the end of each command's output, git-flow adds a (very helpful) description of what it just did. When you need help about a command up front you can always request help, e.g.:

```
$ git flow feature help
```

By starting a feature like this, git-flow created a new branch called "feature/rss-feed" (the "feature/" prefix was one of the configurable options on setup). As you already know, using separate branches for your feature development is one of the most important ground rules in version control.

git-flow also directly checks out the new branch so you can jump right into work.

Finishing a Feature

After some time of hard work and a number of clever commits, our feature is finally done:

```
$ git flow feature finish rss-feed
Switched to branch 'develop'
Updating 6bcf266..41748ad
Fast-forward
    feed.xml | 0
    1 file changed, 0 insertions(+), 0 deletions(-)
    create mode 100644 feed.xml
Deleted branch feature/rss-feed (was 41748ad).
```

Most importantly, the "feature finish" command integrates our work back into the main "develop" branch. There, it waits...

1. ...to be thouroughly tested in the broader "develop" context.

2. ...to be released at a later time with all the other features that accumulate in the "develop" branch.

git-flow also cleans up after us: it deletes the (now obsolete) feature branch and checks out the "develop" branch.

Managing Releases

Release management is another important topic that version control deals with. Let's look at how to create and publish releases with git-flow.

Creating a New Release

Do you feel that your current code on the "develop" branch is ripe for a new release? This should mean that it (a) contains all the new features and fixes and (b) has been thoroughly tested. If both (a) and (b) are true, you're ready to start a new release:

```
$ git flow release start 1.1.5
Switched to a new branch 'release/1.1.5'
```

Note that release branches are named using version numbers. In addition to being an obvious choice, this naming scheme has a a nice side-effect: git-flow can automatically tag the release commit appropriately when we later finish the release.

With a new release branch in place, popular last preparations include bumping the version number (if your type of project keeps note of the version number somewhere in a file) and making any last-minute adaptions.

Finishing the Release

It's time to hit the red danger button and finish our release:

```
git flow release finish 1.1.5
```

This triggers a couple of actions:

1. First, git-flow pulls from the remote repository to make sure you are up-to-date.

2. Then, the release content is merged back into both "master" and "develop" (so that not only the production code is up-to-date, but also new feature branches will be based off the latest code).

3. To easily identify and reference it later, the release commit is tagged with the release's name ("1.1.5" in our case).

4. To clean up, the release branch is deleted and we're back on "develop".

From Git's point of view, the release is now finished. Depending on your set-up, committing on "master" might have already triggered your deployment process - or you now manually do anything necessary to get your software product into the hands of your users.

Hotfixes

As thoroughly tested as your releases might be: all too often, just a couple of hours or days later, a little bug might nonetheless show its antennas. For cases like these, git-flow offers the special "hotfix" workflow (since neither a "feature" branch nor a "release" branch would be appropriate).

Creating Hotfixes

```
$ git flow hotfix start missing-link
```

This creates a new branch named "hotfix/missing-link". Since we need to fix production code, the hotfix branch is based off of "master".

This is also the most obvious distinction from release branches, which are based off of the "develop" branch. Because you wouldn't want to base a production hotfix on your (still unstable) develop code...

Just like with a release, however, we bump up our project's version number and - of course - fix that bug!

Finishing Hotfixes

With our solution committed to the hotfix branch, it's time to wrap up:

```
$ git flow hotfix finish missing-link
```

The procedure is very similar to finishing a release:

› The changes are merged both into "master" as well as into "develop" (to make sure the bug doesn't slip into the next release, again).

› The hotfix is tagged for easy reference.

› The branch is deleted and "develop" is checked out again.

As with a release, now's the time to build / deploy your product (in case this hasn't already been triggered automatically).

Workflows: A Recap

Let me finish this chapter by stressing an important point once more: git-flow doesn't add any functionality on top of Git. It's simply a set of scripts that bundle Git commands into workflows.

However, agreeing on a fixed process makes collaborating in a team much easier: everybody, from the "Git pro" to the "version control newbie", knows how certain tasks ought to be done.

Keep in mind, though, that you don't have to use git-flow to achieve this: often, after some time and experience, teams notice that they don't need git-flow anymore. Once the basic parts and goals of a workflow are understood, you're free to define your own.

Handling Large Files with LFS

Working with large binary files can be quite a hassle: they bloat your local repository and leave you with Gigabytes of data on your machine. Most annoyingly, the majority of this huge amount of data is probably useless for you: most of the time, you don't need *each and every version* of a file on your disk.

This problem in mind, Git's standard feature set was enhanced with the "Large File Storage" extension - in short: "Git LFS". An LFS-enhanced *local* Git repository will be significantly smaller in size because it breaks one basic rule of Git in an elegant way: it does *not* keep *all* of the project's data in your local repository.

Let's look at how this works.

Only the Data You Need

Let's say you have a 100 MB Photoshop file in your project. When you make a change to this file (no matter how tiny it might be), committing this modification will save the *complete* file (huge as it is) in your repository. After a couple of iterations, your local repository will quickly weigh tons of Megabytes and soon Gigabytes.

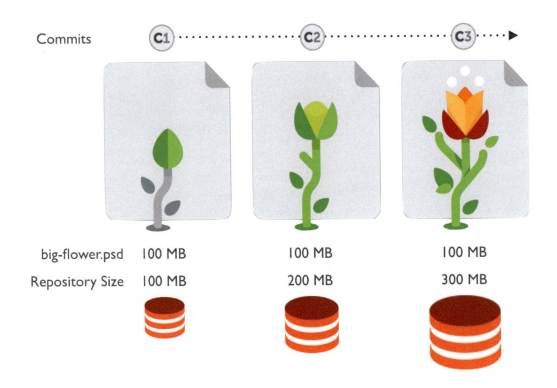

When a coworker clones that repository to her local machine, she will need to download a huge amount of data. And, as already mentioned, most of this data will be of little value: usually, old versions of files aren't used on a daily basis - but they still weigh a lot of Megabytes...

The LFS extension uses a simple technique to avoid your local Git repository from exploding like that: **it does not keep all versions of a file on your machine**. Instead, it only provides the files you actually **need** in your checked out revision. If you switch branches, it will automatically check if you need a specific version of such a big file and get it for you - on demand.

Pointers Instead of Real Data

But what exactly *is* stored in your local repository? We already heard that, in terms of **actual files**, only those items are present that are actually needed in the currently checked out revision. But what about the other versions of an LFS-managed file?

To do its size-reducing wonders, LFS only stores **pointers** to these files in the repository. These pointers are just references to the actual files which are stored elsewhere, in a special **LFS store**.

An Additional Object Store

The usual Git setup is probably old hat to you:

› Your local computer is home to a *local Git repository* and the project's *Working Copy*.

› Most likely (although not mandatory) there's also a remote server involved which hosts the *remote repository*.

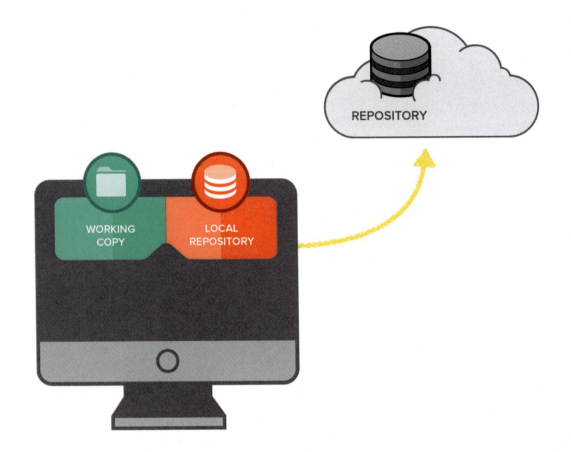

With LFS, this classic setup is extended by an *LFS cache* and an *LFS store*:

> Remember that an LFS-tracked file is only saved as a *pointer* in the repository. The actual file data, therefore, has to be located somewhere else: in the *LFS cache* that now accompanies your local Git repository.

> On the remote side of things, an *LFS store* saves and delivers all of those large files on demand.

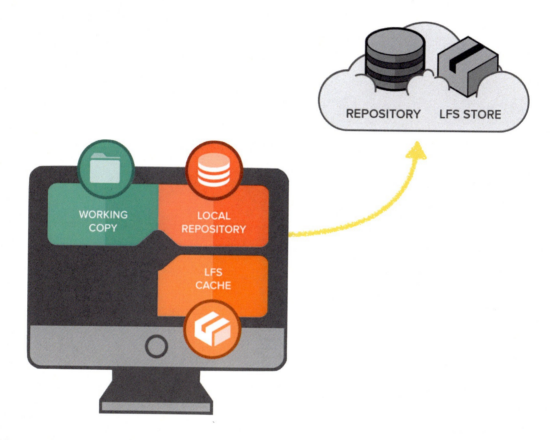

Whenever Git in your local repository encounters an LFS-managed file, it will only find a pointer - not the file's actual data. It will then ask the local LFS Cache to deliver it. The LFS Cache tries to look up the file by its pointer; if it doesn't have it already, it requests it from the remote LFS Store.

That way, you only have the file data on disk that is *necessary* for you at the moment. Everything else will be downloaded on demand.

Before we get our hands dirty installing and actually *using* LFS there's one last thing to do: please check if your code hosting service of choice supports LFS.

Although most popular services like GitHub, GitLab, and Visual Studio already offer support for LFS, it's nothing to take for granted.

Installing Git LFS

LFS is a fairly recent invention and not (yet) part of the core Git feature set. It's provided as an extension that you'll have to install once on your local machine.

Installation is quick and simple:

> Linux: Debian and RPM packages are available from PackageCloud (https://packagecloud.io/github/git-lfs/install).

> macOS: You can either use Homebrew (https://github.com/Homebrew/brew) via "brew install git-lfs" or MacPorts (https://www.macports.org) via "port install git-lfs".

> Windows: Use the Chocolatey (https://chocolatey.org) package manager via "choco install git-lfs".

To finish the installation, you need to run the "install" command once to complete the initialization:

```
git lfs install
```

CONCEPT

Good news if you're using the Tower desktop GUI: all recent versions of the app already include LFS. You don't have to install anything else!

Tracking a File with LFS

Out of the box, LFS doesn't do anything with your files: you have to **explicitly tell** it which files it should track!

Let's start by adding a large file to the repository, e.g. a nice 100 MB Photoshop file:

With the "track" command, you can tell LFS to take care of the file:

```
git lfs track "design.psd"
```

If you expected fireworks to go off, you'll probably be a bit disappointed: the command didn't do much. But you'll notice that the ".gitattributes" file in the root of your project was changed! This is where Git LFS remembers which files it should track.

If we look at it now, we'll be happy to see that LFS made an entry about our "design.psd" file:

```
design.psd filter=lfs diff=lfs merge=lfs -text
```

Just like the ".gitignore" file (responsible for ignoring items), the ".gitattributes" file and any changes that happen to it should be included in version control. Put simply, you should commit changes to ".gitattributes" to the repository like any other changes, too:

```
git add .gitattributes
git add design.psd
git commit -m "Add design file"
```

Tracking Patterns

It would be a bit tedious if you had to *manually* tell LFS about every single file you want to track. That's why you can feed it a file pattern instead of the path of a particular file. As an example, let's tell LFS to track all ".mov" files in our repository:

```
git lfs track "*.mov"
```

To avoid some slippery slopes, keep two things in mind when creating a new tracking rule:

› Don't forget the quotes around the file pattern. It indeed makes a difference if you write **git lfs track "*.mov"** or **git lfs track *.mov**. In the latter case, the command line will expand the wildcard and create individual rules for all .mov files in your project - which you probably do *not* want!

› Always execute the "track" command from the root of your project. The reason for this advice is that patterns are relative to the folder in which you ran the command. Keep things simple and always use it from the repository's root folder.

Which Files Are We Tracking

At some point, you might want to check which files in your project you are *effectively* tracking via Git LFS. This is where the "ls-files" command comes in handy: it lists all of the files that are tracked by LFS in the current working copy.

```
git lfs ls-files
3515fd8462 * design.psd
```

Whenever you're in doubt if a certain file is *really* managed by LFS, simply assure yourself with the "ls-files" command.

When to Track

You can accuse Git of many things - but definitely not of forgetfulness: things that you've committed to the repository are there to stay. It's very hard to get things out of a project's commit history (and that's a good thing).

In the end, this means one thing: make sure to set your LFS tracking patterns as early as possible - ideally right after initializing a new repository. To change a file that was committed the usual way into an LFS-managed object, you would have to manipulate and rewrite your project's history. And you certainly want to avoid this.

Cloning a Git LFS Repository

To clone an existing LFS repository from a remote server, you can simply use the standard "git clone" command that you already know. After downloading the repository, Git will check out the default branch and then hand over to LFS: if there are any LFS-managed files in the current revision, they'll be automatically downloaded for you.

That's all well and good - but if you want to speed up the cloning process, you can also use the "git lfs clone" command instead. The main difference is that, after the initial checkout was performed, the requested LFS items are downloaded *in parallel* (instead of one after the other). This could be a nice time saver for repositories with lots of LFS-tracked files.

Working with Your Repository

Undeniably, the best part about Git LFS is that it doesn't require you to change your workflow. Apart from telling LFS which files it should track, there is nothing to watch out for! No matter if it's committing, pushing or pulling: you can continue to work with the commands you already know and use.

Authentication with SSH Public Keys

Often, access to a remote Git repository on a server will be restricted: you probably don't want to allow anybody to read (or at least not write to) your files. In these cases, some kind of authentication is necessary.

One possibility to authenticate uses the "HTTPS" protocol which you probably already know from your browser. Although this is very easy to use, a lot of system administrators use the also very common "SSH" protocol for various reasons. In this scenario, when it comes to authentication, you will most likely meet "SSH Public Keys".

For this type of authentication, a two-part key is used: a public and a private one. The private key (as the name implies) must be kept absolutely private to you under all circumstances. Its public counterpart, in contrast, is supposed to be installed on all servers that you want to get access to.

› When a connection via SSH is trying to be established, the server will only grant access if it has a public key installed that matches the private key of the requesting computer.

› Should the library change (because bugs were fixed or new features added), we'll have a hard time updating the library code. Again, we need to download the raw files and replace the original items.

Since these are quite common problems in everyday projects, Git of course offers a solution: Submodules.

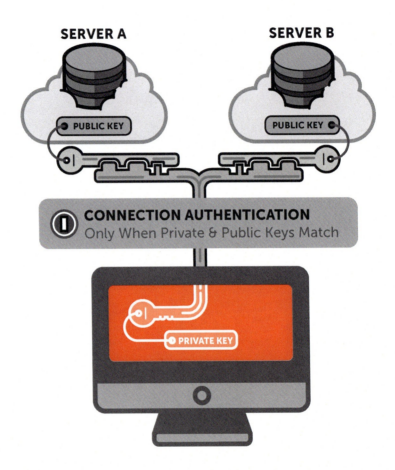

Creating a Public Key

Before creating a public key, you should check if you already have one:

```
$ ls ~/.ssh
```

If a file named "**id_rsa.pub**" or "**id_dsa.pub**" is listed, you already have a key. In this case, you are good to give this file to your
server's administrator or (in case you're using a hosting service like GitHub or Beanstalk) upload it to your account.

Otherwise, creating a key is just a matter of executing a single command:

```
$ ssh-keygen -t rsa -C "john@example.com"
```

With the "-t" flag, we demand an "RSA" type key, which is one of the newest and safest types. With the "-C" flag, we provide a comment which you can think of as a kind of description or label for this key. Using your email address, e.g., lets you identify it more easily later.

After confirming this command, you'll be asked to:

5. Enter a name for this new key. Just hit RETURN to accept the default name and location.

6. Provide a passphrase. Although SSH public key authentication can be used safely without any password, you should nonetheless enter a strong passphrase to enhance security even further.

```
$ ssh-keygen -t rsa -C "john@example.com"
Generating public/private rsa key pair.
Enter file in which to save the key (/Users/tobidobi/.ssh/id_rsa):
Enter passphrase (empty for no passphrase):
Enter same passphrase again:
Your identification has been saved in /Users/tobidobi/.ssh/id_rsa.
Your public key has been saved in /Users/tobidobi/.ssh/id_rsa.pub.
The key fingerprint is:
87:23:34:de:35:d0:f2:78:05:a4:78:1b:f1:6a:7e:be john@example.com
The key's randomart image is:
+--[ RSA 2048]----+
|     . = o       |
|    ..o..        |
|   . o S .       |
| . .        . o  |
| . + + . o       |
|  . S = + o.     |
|    . . + + . o  |
|       o .       |
|            o .  |
|            .Eo  |
+-----------------+
```

Now, two files will have been created for you: "id_rsa.pub" (your public key) and "id_rsa" (your private key). If you're on a Mac, you'll find these in the ".ssh" folder inside your home directory (~./ssh/). On Windows, you should look in C:\Documents and Settings\your-username\.ssh\ or C:\Users\your-user-name\.ssh.

If you take a look at the actual contents of your public key file, you'll see something like this:

```
$ cat ~/.ssh/id_rsa.pub
ssh-rsa AAAB3nZaC1aycAAEU+/ZdulUJoeuchOUU02/j18L7fo+ltQ0f322+Au/9yy9oaAB-
BRCrHN/yo88BC0AB3nZaC1aycAAEU+/ZdulUJoeuchOUU02/j18L7fo+ltQ0f322AB3nZaC1ay-
cAAEU+/ZdulUJoeuchOUU02/j18L7fo+ltQ0f322AB3nZaC1aycAAEU+/ZdulUJoeuchOUU02/
j18L7fo+ltQ0f322AB3nZaC1aycAAEU+/ZdulUJoeuchOUU02/j18L7fo+ltQ0f322klCi0/
aEBBc02N+JJP john@example.com
```

It's this output that needs to be installed on the remote server you want to get access to. In case you have an own server for your team, you'll give this to your server's administrator. In case you're using a code hosting service like GitHub or Beanstalk, you'll have to upload this to your account.

You have to copy the content of the public key file exactly as it is - no whitespace or the like is accepted. To make this as safe and easy as possible, you can use the following command to have this copied to your clipboard:

```
$ pbcopy < ~/.ssh/id_rsa.pub          [on Mac]
$ clip < ~/.ssh/id_rsa.pub            [on Windows]
```

CHAPTER 5:
TOOLS & SERVICES

Desktop GUIs

You've learned quite a lot of Git commands in the course of this book. Although this is indispensable in the learning process, version control is not about learning all of the commands and parameters by heart.

As soon as you have a basic understanding, switching to a desktop GUI application can make your life a lot easier. Especially the fact that it provides you with a visual representation of everything is a huge help.

A lot of tasks can be performed easier and more comfortably using a desktop application. Let alone not having to memorize dozens of commands (including their syntax and parameters).

A good GUI application will make you more productive and give you the confidence to use all of Git's advantages.

Tower Git Client

As the makers of Tower (http://www.git-tower.com), we'd love if you gave it a try. It's popular among both individual software developers and companies like Apple, Google, Amazon, Ebay, and Twitter.

With its easy-to-use interface, the application focuses on taking the complexity out of Git, while still offering all of the advanced features.

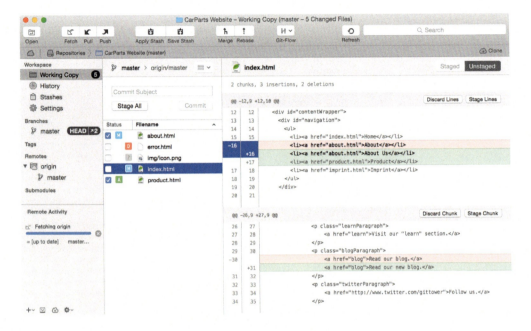

The "Working Copy" view shows you which files you modified, how you modified them, and which files are staged for the next commit.

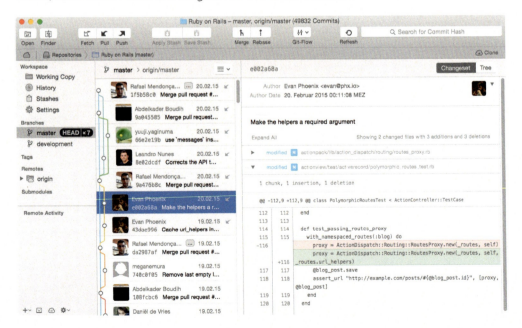

The "History" view provides a perfect overview everything there is to know about a certain commit - including e.g. integrated file diff information.

It's available for both Mac OS and Windows. You can try it free for 30 days: http://www.git-tower.com

Diff & Merge Tools

To understand what happened in a project, you need to inspect changes. And since changes are represented as "diffs", it's crucial to be able to understand these diffs.

While the command line is the easiest way to output diff data, it can't go very far in making it **easy to read**:

```
$ git diff
diff --git a/css/about.css b/css/about.css
index e69de29..4b5800f 100644
--- a/css/about.css
+++ b/css/about.css
@@ -0,0 +1,2 @@
+h1 {
+   line-height:30px; }
\ No newline at end of file
diff --git a/css/general.css b/css/general.css
index a3b8935..d472b7f 100644
--- a/css/general.css
+++ b/css/general.css
@@ -21,7 +21,8 @@ body {

  h1, h2, h3, h4, h5 {
     color:#ffd84c;
-    font-family: "Trebuchet MS", "Trebuchet"; }
+    font-family: "Trebuchet MS", "Trebuchet";
+    margin-bottom:0px; }


  p {
     margin-bottom:6px;}
diff --git a/error.html b/error.html
deleted file mode 100644
index 78a1c33..0000000
--- a/error.html
+++ /dev/null
@@ -1,43 +0,0 @@
- <html>
-
-    <head>
-        <title>
-
```

A diff tool application, in contrast, is dedicated to just this single job: helping you understand diffs more easily. It uses colors, special formatting, and even different arrangements (side-by-side, combined in a single column, etc.) to achieve this:

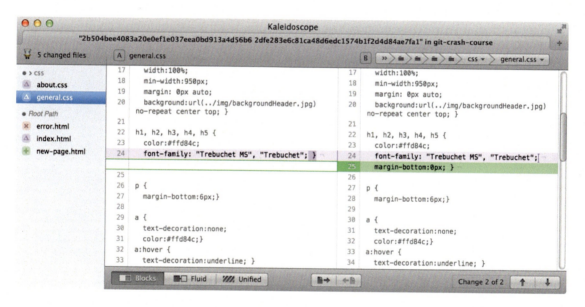

Some of these tools can even help you solve merge conflicts. Especially in this situation, you'll quickly come to appreciate a tool that helps reduce complexity and avoid mistakes.

Today, there are lots of great tools on the market. Below is a short list to give you an overview.

macOS

- Kaleidoscope: www.kaleidoscopeapp.com

- Araxis Merge: www.araxis.com

- DeltaWalker: www.deltopia.com

Windows

- BeyondCompare www.scootersoftware.com

- Araxis Merge: www.araxis.com

- P4Merge: www.perforce.com

Code Hosting Services

Hosting your code becomes an important topic as soon as you want to start sharing it – and be it only with yourself on another machine. There are basically two different flavors of code hosting: do-it-yourself and leave-me-in-peace.

(A) Do-It-Yourself

Hosting a Git repository on your own server has a lot of advantages:

› It saves money you'd have to spend on code hosting services.

› It keeps your code in-house.

› And it generally gives you all the freedom in the world.

But, of course, this also comes with some drawbacks:

› YOU are responsible for ensuring high availability / up-time of the server.

› YOU are responsible for making backups (that really, really work).

› YOU are responsible for keeping an eye on security and software updates.

In the end, the hard part about hosting code is not the management of the Git repositories. It's the management and maintenance of the server. Don't get me wrong: the bottom line is NOT "stop hosting code yourself and use a code hosting service". The bottom line is "be aware of what hosting your code yourself really means".

If you have enough expertise doing this yourself and if you're willing to invest the time, hosting your repositories on your own server is perfect for you!

(B) Leave-Me-In-Peace

For most people, their core competence is not server maintenance. While a lot of people _theoretically have the knowledge_ to do it themselves, they're often not proficient enough for this to make sense.

By now, there are dozens of specialized service providers available that do all the server management, backup, and security stuff for you. We've compiled a short list of some of them to give you a quick overview.

GitHub (www.github.com)

GitHub is the most popular code hosting service in the Git world. Especially for OpenSource projects, GitHub is the go-to platform.

Beanstalk (www.beanstalkapp.com)

Beanstalk offers hosting not only for Git repositories, but also for Subversion projects. Being a very lean and reliable service, Beanstalk is a great choice for businesses.

Bitbucket (www.bitbucket.com)

Besides Git repositories, Bitbucket also offers hosting for the Mercurial VCS. It has a similar feature set as the GitHub platform, although it's not as popular in the OpenSource space.

Plan.io (www.plan.io)

Plan.io offers a complete project management platform. In addition to code hosting (Git and Subversion), it also provides you with modules for task management, customer helpdesk, and even integrated Wikis.

CLOSING
THOUGHTS

State of Play

Reaching this part of the book (assuming that you haven't started reading from the end...), you should pat yourself on the back: not only do you now master the basics of version control; you also picked Git, one of the most promising systems, as your tool of choice. My sincerest congratulations!

But the journey doesn't have to end here. You're now in a good position to build on your basic knowledge and move forward.

Learning Resources

In recent years, the amount of documentation, tutorials, and articles on Git has increased a lot, fortunately. I recommend you have a look at the following resources:

- "Git - the Simple Guide": http://rogerdudler.github.io/git-guide/
- Cheat Sheet: https://www.git-tower.com/learn/cheat-sheets/git
- Video Course: https://www.git-tower.com/learn/git/videos/

APPENDIX

Appendix A: Version Control Best Practices

Commit Related Changes

A commit should be a wrapper for related changes. For example, fixing two different bugs should produce two separate commits. Small commits make it easier for other team members to understand the changes and roll them back if something went wrong. With tools like the staging area and the ability to stage only parts of a file, Git makes it easy to create very granular commits.

Commit Often

Committing often keeps your commits small and, again, helps you commit only related changes. Moreover, it allows you to share your code more frequently with others. That way it's easier for everyone to integrate changes regularly and avoid having merge conflicts. Having few large commits and sharing them rarely, in contrast, makes it hard both to solve conflicts and to comprehend what happened.

Don't Commit Half-Done Work

You should only commit code when it's completed. This doesn't mean you have to complete a whole, large feature before committing. Quite the contrary: split the feature's implementation into logical chunks and remember to commit early and often. But don't commit just to have something in the repository before leaving the office at the end of the day. If you're tempted to commit just because you need a clean working copy (to check out a branch, pull in changes, etc.) consider using Git's "Stash" feature instead.

Test Before You Commit

Resist the temptation to commit something that you "think" is completed. Test it thoroughly to make sure it really is completed and has no side effects (as far as one can tell). While committing half-baked things in your local repository only requires you to forgive yourself, having your code tested is even more important when it comes to pushing / sharing your code with others.

Write Good Commit Messages

Begin your message with a short summary of your changes (up to 50 characters as a guideline). Separate it from the following body by including a blank line. The body of your message should provide detailed answers to the following questions: What was the motivation for the change? How does it differ from the previous implementation? Use the imperative, present tense ("change", not "changed" or "changes") to be consistent with generated messages from commands like git merge.

Version Control is not a Backup System

Having your files backed up on a remote server is a nice side effect of having a version control system. But you should not use your VCS like it was a backup system. When doing version control, you should pay attention to committing semantically (see "related changes") – you shouldn't just cram in files.

Use Branches

Branching is one of Git's most powerful features – and this is not by accident: quick and easy branching was a central requirement from day one. Branches are the perfect tool to help you avoid mixing up different lines of development. You should use branches extensively in your development workflows: for new features, bug fixes, experiments, ideas...

Agree on a Workflow

Git lets you pick from a lot of different workflows: long-running branches, topic branches, merge or rebase, git-flow... Which one you choose depends on a couple of factors: your project, your overall development and deployment workflows and (maybe most importantly) on your and your teammates' personal preferences. However you choose to work, just make sure to agree on a common workflow that everyone follows.

Appendix B: Command Line 101

For many non-technical people, the command line (also referred to as CLI, Terminal, bash, or shell) is a place of mystery. However, you only have to know a handful of basic commands to start feeling comfortable.

Opening Your Command Line Interface

On a Mac, the most common application for command line gymnastics is "Terminal.app". It comes pre-installed with every Mac OS X system. You'll find it in the "Applications" folder, inside the "Utilities" subfolder.

On Windows, following the installation guidelines earlier in this book will provide you with an application called "Git Bash". You'll find it in your Windows START menu, inside the "Git" folder.

Finding Your Way Around

As the name already implies, the command line is used to execute commands: you type something and confirm the command by hitting ENTER. Most of these commands are dependent on your current location - where "location" means a certain directory or path on your computer.

So, let's issue our first command to find out where we currently are:

```
$ pwd
```

You can easily remember this command when you know what it stands for: "**p**rint **w**orking **d**irectory". It will return the path to a local folder on your computer's disk.

To change this current working directory, you can use the "cd" command (where "cd" stands for "**c**hange **d**irectory"). For example, to move one directory upwards (into the current folder's parent folder), you can just call:

```
$ cd ..
```

To move into subfolders, you would call something like this:

```
$ cd name-of-subfolder/sub-subfolder/
```

Often, you'll see a special kind of path notation: "~". This sign stands for your user account's home folder. So, instead of typing something like "cd /Users/<your-username>/", you should use this shorthand form:

```
$ cd ~/projects/
```

Also very important is the "ls" command that lists the file contents of a directory. I suggest you always use this command with two additional options: "-l" formats the output list a little more structured and "-a" also lists "hidden" files (which is helpful when working with version control). Showing the contents of the current directory works as follows:

```
$ ls -la
```

Working with Files

The most important file operations can be controlled with just a handful of commands.

Let's start by removing a file:

```
$ rm path/to/file.ext
```

When trying to delete a folder, however, please note that you'll have to add the "-r" flag (which stand for "recursive"):

```
$ rm -r path/to/folder
```

Moving a file is just as simple:

```
$ mv path/to/file.ext different/path/file.ext
```

The "mv" command can also be used to rename a file:

```
$ mv old-filename.ext new-filename.ext
```

If, instead of moving the file, you want to copy it, simply use "cp" instead of "mv".

Finally, to create a new folder, you call the "make directory" command:

```
$ mkdir new-folder
```

Generating Output

The command line is quite an all-rounder: it can also display a file's contents - although it won't do this as elegantly as your favorite editor. Nonetheless, there are cases where it's handy to use the command line for this. For example when you only want to take a quick look - or when GUI apps are simply not available because you're working on a remote server.

The "cat" command outputs the whole file in one go:

```
$ cat file.ext
```

In a similar way, the "head" command displays the file's first 10 lines, while "tail" shows the last 10 lines. You can simply scroll up and down in the output like you're used to from other applications.

The "less" command is a little different in this regard.

```
$ less file.ext
```

Although it's also used to display output, it controls page flow itself. This means that it only displays one page full of content and then waits for your explicit instructions. You'll know you have "less" in front of you if the last line of your screen either shows the file's name or just a colon (":") that waits to receive orders from you.

Hitting SPACE will scroll one page forward, "b" will scroll one page backward, and "q" will simply quit the "less" program.

Making Your Life Easier on the Command Line

There's a handful of little tricks that make your life a lot easier while working with the command line.

TAB Key

Whenever you're entering file names (including paths to a file or directory), the **TAB** key comes in very handy. It autocompletes what you've written, which reduces typos very efficiently. For example, when you want to switch to a different directory, you can either type every component of the path yourself:

```
$ cd ~/projects/acmedesign/documentation/
```

Or you make use of the **TAB** key (try this yourself!):

```
$ cd ~/pr[TAB]ojects/ac[TAB]medesign/doc[TAB]umentation/
```

In case your typed characters are ambiguous (because "dev" could be the "development" or the "developers" folder...), the command line won't be able to autocomplete. In that case, you can hit **TAB** another time to get all the possible matches shown and can then type a few more characters.

ARROW Keys

The command line keeps a history of the most recent commands you executed. By pressing the **ARROW UP** key, you can step through the last commands you called (starting with the most recently used). **ARROW DOWN** will move forward in history towards the most recent call.

CTRL Key

When entering commands, pressing **CTRL+A** moves the caret to the beginning of the line, while **CTRL+E** moves it to the end of the line.

Finally, not all commands are finished by simply submitting them: some require further inputs from you after hitting return. In case you should ever be stuck in the middle of a command and want to abort it, hitting **CTRL+C** will cancel that command. While this is safe to do in most situations, please note that aborting a command can of course leave things in an unsteady state.

Appendix C: Switching from Subversion to Git

Actually, switching from Subversion to Git isn't very complicated - but only if you don't treat Git like a fancier Subversion. Once you understand where the concepts differ, the transition becomes easy.

Distributed vs. Centralized

Subversion is a **centralized** version control system: all team members work towards a single central repository, placed on a remote server. A "checkout" from this central repository will place a "working copy" on the user's machine. This is a snapshot from a certain version of the project on his disk.

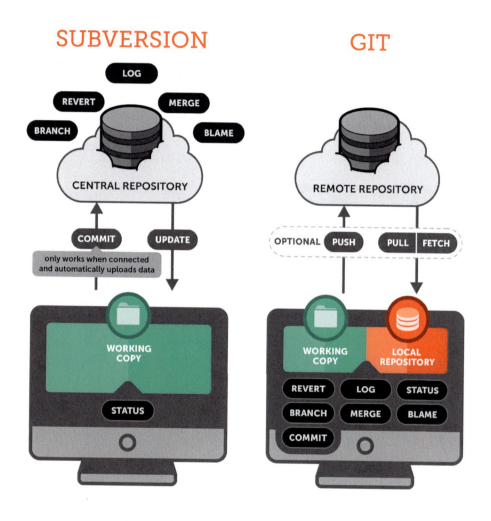

In Git, a distributed version control system, things work a little differently. Instead of a "checkout", a Git user will "clone" a repository from a remote server. In return, he receives a full-fledged repository, not just a working copy. The user then has his own repository on his local machine - including all of the project's history.

You can do everything on your local machine: commit, inspect history, re-store older revisions, etc. Only if you want to share your work with the world you have to connect to a remote server.

Repository Structure and URLs

A Subversion repository is typically organized with a couple of directories: "trunk" for the main line of development, "branches" for alternative contexts, and "tags" to mark certain revisions. To address these different parts, URLs are used that point to these locations inside the repository:

```
svn+ssh://svn@example.com/svn/trunk
```

Git repositories, on the other hand, consist of only a single ".git" folder in the root of a project. Addressing branches or tags is done via commands, not URLs. In Git, the URL only points to the location of the Git repository.

```
ssh://git@example.com/path/to/git-repo.git
```

Branching

As just mentioned, branches in Subversion are just simple directories that happen to have a special meaning. When creating a new branch, you effectively create a (very efficient) copy of your project in a new folder.

In Git, branching was one of the core design goals and therefore required a quite different concept. A branch in Git is simply a pointer to a certain revision - thereby creating no copy, no new directories, and no overhead.
You are **always** working on a branch in Git, even if it's just the default "master"

branch that gets created automatically. Your working directory contains the files that belong to this currently active branch (in Git called the "HEAD"). All other versions and branches are stored in your local repository, ready to be restored in an instant.

Also keep in mind the distributed nature of Git: branches can exist remotely **and** - much more important for your daily work - locally.

Committing

When making a commit in Subversion, a couple of rules apply:

> You can only commit when you have a connection to the central repository. You can't commit while you're offline.

> The commit gets instantly transferred to the central repository.

> It gets assigned an ascending revision number.

Committing in Git differs in some aspects:

> You don't have to be online or connected to any "central" repository - because you have a full-blown repository on your local disk. Therefore, commits are recorded only in your local repository. They're not transferred to any remote repository until you explicitly decide to share them.

> Only because a file was changed doesn't mean it will automatically be included in the next commit. You have to explicitly mark the changes you want in the next commit by adding them to the so-called "Staging Area". You can even mark parts or individual lines of a file to be included, while other parts are left for a later commit.

> Revision numbers are replaced by "commit hashes". Since commits happen offline on the developers' local machines, you cannot assign one commit #5 and another one #6 - who's first in such a distributed scenario? However, of course, there must still be a way to uniquely identify commits in Git. Therefore, a hashed string is used instead of the ascending revision number.

Sharing Work

With Subversion, your work is automatically transferred to the central server when you commit. And committing is only possible when you can connect to this central server.

In Git, nothing gets uploaded automatically. You can decide for each of your branches when (and if at all) you want to share them with your team. Besides that, sharing work is very safe: conflicts can only occur on your local machine and not on the remote server. This leaves you with the confidence that you cannot break things.

Appendix D: Why Git?

Although there are dozens of version control systems on the market, some of the world's most renowned projects (like the Linux Kernel, Ruby on Rails, or jQuery) are using Git as their VCS of choice. Here are some of the reasons why.

Save Time

Git is lightning fast. And although we're talking about only a few seconds per command, it quickly adds up in your work day. Use your time for something more useful than waiting for your version control system to get back to you.

Work Offline

What if you want to work while you're on the move? With a centralized VCS like Subversion or CVS, you're stranded if you're not connected to the central repository. With Git, almost everything is possible simply on your local machine: make a commit, browse your project's complete history, merge or create branches... Git let's you decide where and when you want to work.

Undo Mistakes

People make mistakes. A good thing about Git is that there's a little "undo" command for almost every situation. Correct your last commit because you forgot to include that small change. Revert a whole commit because that feature isn't necessary, anymore. And when the going gets tough you can even restore disappeared commits with the Reflog - because, behind the scenes, Git rarely really deletes something. This is peace of mind.

Don't Worry

Git gives you the confidence that you can't screw things up - and this is a great feeling. In Git, every clone of a project that one of your teammates might have on his local computer is a fully usable backup. Additionally, almost every action in Git only adds data (deleting is very rare). That means that losing data or breaking a repository beyond repair is really hard to do.

Make Useful Commits

A commit is only really useful if it just contains related changes. Imagine having a commit that contains something from feature A, a little bit of feature B, and bugfix C. This is hard to understand for your teammates and can't be rolled back easily if some of the code is causing problems. Git helps you create granular commits with its unique "staging area" concept: you can determine exactly which changes shall be included in your next commits, even down to single lines. This is where version control starts to be useful.

Work in Your Own Way

When working with Git you can use your very own workflow. One that feels good for you. You don't have to be a code acrobat to qualify for using Git. Of course, you can connect with multiple remote repositories, rebase instead of merge, and work with submodules when you need it. But you can just as easily work with one central remote repository like in Subversion. All the other advantages remain – regardless of your workflow.

Don't Mix Things Up

Separation of concerns is paramount to keeping track of things. While you're working on feature A, nothing (and no-one) else should be affected by your unfinished code. What if it turns out the feature isn't necessary anymore? Or if, after 10 commits, you notice that you took a completely wrong approach? Branching is the answer for these problems. And while other version control systems also know branches, Git is the first one to make it work as it should: fast & easy.

Go With the Flow

Only dead fish swim with the stream. And sometimes, clever developers do, too. Git is used by more and more well-known companies and Open Source projects: Ruby On Rails, jQuery, Perl, Debian, the Linux Kernel and many more. A large community often is an advantage by itself because an ecosystem evolves around the system. Lots of tutorials, tools, and services make Git even more attractive.

Made in the USA
Lexington, KY
25 July 2018